WILD
LEADERSHIP

WILD
LEADERSHIP

WHAT WILD ANIMALS TEACH US
ABOUT LEADERSHIP

ERNA WALRAVEN

To Robbie.

CONTENTS

INTRODUCTION

In my work as an animal carer, zookeeper and curator, I have been privileged to work with a large and inspiring range of wild animals. More than three decades of observing animals in the wild and under human care has given me much to think about, particularly in terms of social groups and how leadership works in animals. What makes a good leader? Why do animals follow this particular leader? Why are some animal leaders replaced more violently than others? How and why does leadership differ between species and under different circumstances? What are the most common beneficial traits of wild animal leaders and why does any of this matter to us? I share these animal insights hoping that people are encouraged to evaluate their leadership styles in light of the principles we see in nature.

As a young zookeeper in the 1980s it was very much frowned upon to talk about animals having feelings or being driven by emotions. We were to observe and describe what we saw objectively without being anthropomorphic. However, if you work closely with wild animals, as zookeepers do, it is impossible not to identify the emotions you see in them. Spending my days watching and caring for animals, I saw regret, love, mistrust, jealousy, envy, embarrassment and all the common sentiments we humans also feel and can recognise in other humans. What a relief it was to have Frans de Waal publish his book on *Chimpanzee Politics* in 1982. Finally, there was confirmation of what other zookeepers and I saw daily: some animals plan and plot, they have relationships and they certainly have a wide range of feelings.

Thanks to Frans de Waal and fellow researchers it now seems that science has accepted what many zookeepers and animal carers have long known.

Animals are like us in more ways than we have given them credit for.

The closer we are to the species genetically, the more likely it is we can identify the feelings we see in those animals. So for us, it is naturally easier to understand the sentiments expressed by the great apes, such as orangutans, gorillas, Bonobos or Chimpanzees. However, I have also known birds with a sense of humour, bats with jealousy issues and shy penguins.

In groups of social animals there is usually a hierarchy, with one animal or a pair leading the group. As an animal carer there is usually little you can do when the animals in your care undergo a change of leadership. Animals will follow their own instincts and choose or support the leader they want. Leadership changes can be violent and quite harmful to the leader being overthrown. Observing this at close quarters over many years led me to think a lot about leadership, its 'hows' and 'whys'. At the same time, the more I read and understood about evolutionary biology, the more I appreciated our similarities with other species. Rather than focusing on the differences as society often does, I saw the parallels. We are a species that prefers to think itself superior to all others and we're keen to emphasise difference rather than acknowledge resemblance. As an animal carer for several decades I can't help but see our species reflected in the animals I care for and observe. Boy teenagers pushing and jostling each other at the corner of the shopping centre remind me of young and boisterous bull elephants at an African waterhole, their bravado and mock fighting exploring 'who is the toughest?'. The way teenage girls walk past those same boys in twos or threes, looking but not looking, is reminiscent of female grouse nonchalantly inspecting the male birds on their display ground.

From an evolutionary point of view, we are related equally to the Chimpanzee and the Bonobo, two very different great apes although similar in appearance. While chimps are highly excitable, slightly aggressive, posturing beings, the Bonobo are known to be more peace-loving and to resolve conflict with sex rather than violence. We share numerous biological, emotional and behavioural traits with both of these species. In addition, Chimpanzees have male-dominated societies while Bonobos are female-led. Female leaders are not as common in the animal world, but where they do occur it is fascinating to observe the difference from the male model. Males will often have physical leadership battles for dominance while the female alpha position is often gained through respect for experience and knowledge. The case for aggressive human conduct being a result of our 'animal nature' is clearly simplistic, as this example shows. There is so much more we can learn about our own natures and leadership styles by delving deeper into the complexities of animal societies.

In this book I have focused on the positive leadership conduct displayed in the animal kingdom; the behaviours that offer insights into how humans can be more effective leaders. Wild animals have significant expectations of their leaders. They want to trust them. They want to be protected by them, and they want their leaders to make decisions for the greater good of the community. Incompetent or vicious leaders will be deposed by their animal followers as soon as there is a viable alternative. The nastier an animal leader is, the more violent their defeat will be. This book delves into the intriguing lives of animals, their societies and what we can learn about the best examples of their wild leadership styles.

CHAPTER 1

THE HUMAN ANIMAL

'There is no fundamental difference between man and the higher mammals in their mental faculties... The difference in mind between man and the higher animals, great as it is, certainly is one of degree and not of kind.'

CHARLES DARWIN

We are human. We are also apes. More precisely, we are social apes. The fact that science puts us squarely in the 'social' basket is very relevant to leadership. Once animals or people get together to live in communities, leaders and followers emerge. Leadership is needed to defend territory and clan, to keep the peace and to arbitrate in disputes, to share resources (somewhat) fairly and to console the bereaved. Once communities form, there must be rules about how to live together. We need strategies about how to avoid and minimise internal conflict because we may need to fight the enemy together tomorrow or hunt communally to feed the clan. Leaders implement strategies and enforce their society's rules. Leadership and followership are ancient features in human and many other mammalian societies.

This chapter explores our similarities with wild animals, the genes we share and emotions we feel. It looks at why we are social and how being social shapes our society and the expectations we have of our leaders. Human conduct is closely correlated with the behaviours of wild animals. We also share many leadership qualities and follower expectations with animals. Human sociality shares many similarities with the African great apes; particularly gorillas, Chimpanzees and Bonobos. This chapter also touches upon the shared evolutionary heritage between wild mammals and humans. Why might this heritage be informative when we think about natural leadership styles? Our evolutionary heritage and genetic relationship with wild animals give a context from which to explore the leadership qualities of our wilder relatives.

Many people are interested in their family history. It can give a window into where particular talents, likes or dislikes may have been inherited. For example, your great-great-great-grandmother was an accomplished painter and, low and behold, you are an enthusiastic contributor to local art shows. Stronger evidence for genetic determination of human personalities is provided by the many cases of identical twins separated soon after birth who then mature with astonishingly similar jobs and interests, even the choice of spouses. We inherit traits from our ancestors. Not only from our immediate ones like great-great-great-grandparents but also from ancient wild predecessors that lived millions of years ago.

Who are our relatives from way, way back? Modern humans, *Homo sapiens*, have a very close relationship to the other primates, in particular the apes. We share a common forebear with Chimpanzees, Bonobos and gorillas, who lived between eight and six million years ago. Chimpanzees and Bonobos, our cousin species in the animal kingdom, share nearly 99 per cent of our DNA.

Many of us read crime fiction books or watch crime shows on TV. In a relatively short time we've discovered how important DNA can be in solving crimes and scientific problems. We also know that the science of DNA (molecular genetics) can solve questions we could not have even asked previously.

For example: the DNA difference between Chimpanzees and gorillas, the other great ape in Africa, is about 1.6 per cent. Making Chimpanzees more closely related to *us* than they are to gorillas. Interestingly, Chimpanzees, Bonobos *and* humans all show the same 1.6 per cent DNA difference from gorillas. More of a difference yet again: just over 3 per cent distinguishes us *and* the other African apes from the orangutans. All the great apes *and* humans differ from the Rhesus Macaque, a small monkey from Asia, by about seven per cent in their DNA. This illustrates just how close *our* relationship is to Chimpanzees and Bonobos.

What sets us apart from other species? Is it a greater difference than what separates all species from the next? Do these often-minor differences justify our right to dominate them, increasingly to the point of exterminating them? The focus of these investigations is often about identifying what sets us apart from other animals rather than similarities. Of course there are differences. Most of us are not covered in a coat of black hair and humans evolved the ability to walk on two legs more than four million years ago. The great apes are known as 'quadrupedal' (four-footed) although some are capable of walking on two legs for short periods. Walking upright, bipedalism, is usually considered a distinctly human trait.

Other significant human features are a large brain and the ability to make and use tools. In 1960, the now-renowned primate researcher Jane Goodall came across a wild chimp she named 'David Greybeard,' who seemed to strip the leaves from a twig which he then inserted into a termite mound. The termites bit into the twig and, presto, David had modified a twig to 'fish' for termites. This observation made the world aware, for the first time, that species other than humans made and used tools. Although tool-making was once considered a specific human development, we now know that many animals such as primates, sea otters and crows are also capable of doing so. Species demonstrating the ability to make tools are now discovered quite regularly. Every year the list of animal tool makers grows longer. Many of the traits previously seen as specifically human and setting us apart from the animal world have later been discovered not to be the sole domain of humans.

Language in humans is another trait that sets us apart from the other great apes. Many primate observers now agree that body language, gestures and vocalisations in great ape species allow for sophisticated communication.

Darwin's theory of evolution and the much more recent advances in molecular genetics allow us to think more scientifically about the age-old philosophical question of who we are and our origins, offering us a better understanding of our ancient selves. Studies of wild animals and those in human care have contributed to what we know about animal behaviour. We look at our primate cousins and see what drives and motivates them. Some of these motivations are the same or at least similar to ours and many of our reactions to circumstances are also hardwired and instinctive. This knowledge can help us chart the origins of leadership traits, helping us become better leaders.

KNOWING OUR ANCIENT, WILD SELVES

Although most people are well aware of human history it may be useful to do a recap. This can lead to a greater understanding of how our current leadership behaviour correlates with that of our evolutionary ancestors and primate cousins. Evolution is the lengthy process of change by which people originated from ape-like forebears. Robin Dunbar, in his book *Grooming, Gossip and the Evolutionary Language*, defines evolution as 'the outcome of a successful solution to the problem'. Our existence too is the result of our predecessors successfully having solved problems of survival and adaptations to challenging circumstances. They survived at least long enough to have babies and pass on their genes.

Charles Darwin hypothesised that our ancestors left the forests in Africa in favour of the open plains. Along the way our early relatives developed the ability to walk on two legs, a more suitable way of moving about on the savanna. A study by Michael Sockol found that walking upright could have been more energy efficient than quadrupedal knuckle-walking for early ape-like humans.

Exactly why and when early humans stood upright and started moving around on two feet is still being speculated.

Once we did not need arms and hands for locomotion, we could use them for other things, such as holding weapons, making and using tools. This in turn may have encouraged the growth of a bigger, better brain, although a more recent theory is that increased socialising required a larger brain.

The human brain is unusually large. Our brains have tripled in size from early human ancestors to modern humans and are almost six times larger than expected for a placental mammal of our size.

On the plains, our forebears changed their diet which had been largely vegetarian to include more meat. Although some meat is eaten by other primates, the early human practice of hunting and gathering is not known in other primate groups. Our evolution from mostly vegetarians to carnivorous predators is therefore quite unique in the primate world. Desmond Morris in *The Naked Ape* illustrates the way our forebear transformed:

'His whole body, his way of life, was geared to a forest existence, and then suddenly (suddenly in evolutionary terms) he was jettisoned into a world where he could survive only if he began to live like a brainy, weapon-toting wolf.'

In evolutionary terms, these changes in locomotion or diet due to environmental pressures can be rapid – sometimes so fast that the necessary changes to the physical body are not quite complete. I looked after a wide range of species throughout my career and one that stands out as being an example of a species caught halfway through a big evolutionary change is the Binturong (a medium-sized mammal). In contrast to humans, their diet changed from mostly meat to almost vegetarian. Binturongs are taxonomically a carnivore with a carnivore gut and dentition but are now mostly a vegetarian in practice. As a zookeeper you clearly see the results of that: loads of fruit goes into the binturongs and most of it comes out again on the other side, looking fairly similar to when it went in, poorly digested in its short, meat-processing gut. Binturongs like all organisms are in a process of change in response to an environmental pressure to do so.

Our human predecessors took to hunting for meat on the open plains with gusto. They now had their hands free to carry weapons. The larger brain facilitated the making and use of tools and our communication skills helped us to hunt cooperatively. At this time there were some very accomplished hunters out there on the plains of Africa, already filling this ecological niche. Lions, African Wild Dogs, Cheetahs and hyenas for example. These typical carnivore species were eminently better designed for the job, with superior hearing and smell. On top of that these carnivore species had an enhanced physical design for sprinting and long distance running. Humans at this point have *only just* managed to walk upright.

When it came to the killing of their prey, our forebears did not have the teeth or claws that the original African hunting species had either. How did we compete with these talented hunters? We made tools and weapons that replaced the need for teeth and claws – knives, spearheads and poisoned arrows. Primates, us included, do not tend to have a great sense of smell but our vision is quite good, which is a useful attribute for a hunting lifestyle.

Our progress from a forest-dwelling primate to a hunter-gatherer is a long one – an evolutionary path for which we did not seem to be very well designed in terms of speed, hearing, smell or teeth. It seems though that our brain, not our body, was a determining factor in our success. Our lifestyle changes from a forest-dwelling, fruit-eating primate to a socially hunting ape had major implications for communication and cooperation with group members. This increased need for communication meant we had to enhance our vocal skills and like any other ape, we also kept our old skills of reading body language, facial expressions and gestures.

We read the faces of others and get immediate feedback on how our words or actions are perceived. Chimps and Bonobos do the same. Their facial expressions have been studied in much detail and these expressions make it very clear to other chimps what they are thinking. From only a quick glance at a face, humans are also able to form a judgement – attractive or trustworthy for example. For a social animal it is crucial to assess others quickly. Are they dangerous or friendly? Life itself may depend on that decision.

Chimpanzees also use vocalisations to communicate, mostly described as hoots, grunts, barks, screams and whimpers. Bonobos, too, make many sounds from food calls to long-distance travel peeps, anger and threat calls and a distinct laugh when they play or are tickled. As a communal hunter, we evolved even more vocalisations and are now the most vocal of all the apes. Our language skill is one thing that does *appear* to be unmatched in the animal world.

WHY SOME SPECIES ARE SOCIAL AND OTHERS ARE NOT

Sociality defines us as a species. Sociality is why we need leadership. How wild animals 'make a living' in the wild is diverse. That's what evolution is all about – filling a niche in the ecosystem that can be exploited to ensure survival. Whether an animal species is social or not depends on many things. For example, if the food a species depends on is mostly sparse or far apart there may be a tendency for the species to be solitary. Most cat species are solitary with the notable exception of the lion. If food is abundant and plentiful the animal is more likely to be more social. Many species in dense forest are inclined to being solitary. Species are social so they can warn and defend each other against predators.

The great majority of primate species are social. An exception is the orangutan, another ape closely related to us, with a DNA difference of only 3 per cent. Orangutans feed high in the canopy, where food occurs in small quantities which frequently cannot feed more than one orangutan. This compels orangutans to remain mostly alone and limit their social interactions. Orangutans in human care will share a space with another orangutan, but in my experience this is often done so reluctantly once they have grown to adulthood.

Orangs are known by zookeepers around the world as the deep thinkers amongst the apes. My former colleague, Leif Cocks, founder of The Orangutan Project, cites a well-known saying among zookeepers: 'Give a screwdriver to a chimpanzee and it will throw it at another chimpanzee. Give a screwdriver to a gorilla and it will use it to scratch itself. But give a screwdriver to an orangutan and it will use it to undo the lock.'

Amanda Everett, a great ape keeper at Taronga Zoo with more than 20 years' experience relates a story about a determined female orangutan named Willow:

'I came into the orangutan night-house one morning and Willow had somehow fiddled and fiddled with a stick to unhook the firehose on the wall outside her playroom. She'd pulled the whole thing inside and draped it around the poles and climbing structures in her night yard. She did not want to go outside that day because she was rather pleased with her handiwork.

I had to get a bucket of her favourite foods and negotiate every inch of the fire hose back through the mesh, into the keeper corridor, in exchange for treats. Each time she finished a mouthful she would grab the hose again and hold on tight until I handed over the next piece of food. She knew she was in control, had something I wanted, and she wasn't letting it go without an exchange for something she wanted. Orangutans can be much more focussed on what they want than chimps, for example. A chimp under these circumstances may have lost interest after a couple of minutes, with so many other distractions in their world. Too many other things to do! An orangutan on the other hand is focussed on a goal and will work on it, with great determination, until the job is done.'

There are many species that don't care for the company of others of their kind. Generally, solitary species only get together to mate and procreate. Jaguars don't hang out with other Jaguars to socialise. The only time a Jaguar in the wild is seen with another

Jaguar is during courtship and mating. The female then looks after the young on her own. Later she will chase them from her territory as soon as they are old enough to live independently. Animals that are solitary are often territorial and do not like another animal in their territory, especially an animal of their own kind. They live alone to avoid competition with other members of their species. They will mostly try to avoid each other but when two members of the same solitary species meet they often chase the other off with aggressive displays.

Other examples of solitary species are tigers, leopards, bears, pandas, moose, aardvarks, koalas, badgers and Tasmanian devils. Solitary species such as tigers or orangutans, however dignified and majestic, do not tell us a lot about leadership.

SOCIAL SPECIES NEED COMPANY

As a zookeeper all your working days are concerned with achieving one goal: happy animals. In order to achieve this, what counts first and foremost is the social circumstances the animal is held in. A solitary species does not want company and to give it company could stress it. On the other hand an individual of a social species does not only want company of the same species, it needs it more than almost anything else. So the first thing good zookeepers do is make sure the animals are housed in the best species-appropriate social circumstances that can be provided.

If an animal of a highly social species such as a monkey is, due to unforeseen circumstances, housed on its own, it will most likely be very unhappy. It will show that is not enjoying life by looking depressed, disinterested in food, and losing weight and condition. Its coat may look dull or it may over-groom itself. The solo animal may even get sick and die. When an individual of a social species has to be removed from the group for whatever reason, the main concern is how do we keep them alive until they can be returned to the original family or a new group. Quite often, if a monkey has to be removed from the social group, for say, medical treatment, another monkey, a friend, may be selected to keep it company. This will help reduce the stress in the patient.

For social animals, being with your crowd, even if you are not getting on with them, is still better than being alone. Humans do not do well in solitary confinement, which is why this is used as an additional punishment for people in jail. Humans do much better when we socialise. Research by Susan Pinker, psychologist and the author of *The Village Effect*, finds that there is a strong correlation between social interaction and longevity. Essentially, the better plugged-in we are to our social circle, the longer we are likely to live. There appears to be general consensus amongst researchers and health professionals that people who have social support live longer, have better physical and mental health, and may even reduce their risk of dementia.

Many animals are social to the extent that mothers and offspring bond, and males and females interact to mate. However, the term 'social animal' is usually only applied when there is a level of social organisation that goes beyond this – with permanent groups of adults living together and relationships between individuals enduring from one encounter to another. In the case of social animals, not having those social interactions are not only detrimental to the animal's development, they are crucial.

Members of social species bond together and defend their home or territory. They defend the other members of their social grouping and they care for their young, old and sick. Some use babysitters, have affairs, show joy when babies are born and mourn their dead friends and relatives.

CULTURE IN A GORILLA FAMILY

When the time came for Taronga Zoo to find a new male gorilla for breeding, I consulted extensively with my counterparts in Europe for a suitable candidate. Through the international studbook I identified a short list of 'European' gorilla males of the right age and genetics. Our senior primate keeper, Louise, and I then travelled to Europe to visit each of these males to make sure that we also selected one with the most desirable conduct. After all, he was to lead our family group for many years into the future. The male we selected, Kibali, from a zoo in France, impressed both Louise and me with his calm presence. In a colony of apes in human care, there is often an observable culture in the family group.

We went to see Kibali and his family in France on a winter's day. The gorilla group was inside because of the cold. Sometimes, when a family group is used to more space and has to be inside they can be a bit testy with one another. The Kibali family group was calm and treated each other with respect. Kibali's father, the silverback, was the kind of male we wanted for our group – firm but gentle, with no overt use of aggression to keep control.

The way a silverback leads determines how good a role model he will be for his son. We were very impressed with the father Kibali had grown up with. That was the kind of leader we wanted for our gorilla girls. As soon as we walked in it felt like we knew the group. The way the troop went about its day and behaved with each other was very much the same as our gorilla group in Sydney. It felt like walking into the home of a family that is very much like your own – reassuringly familiar and instantly relatable. So even in a small family of gorillas, a 'culture' can develop, just as it does in our own families or work groups.

PROS AND CONS OF A SOCIAL LIFE

There are benefits *and* disadvantages to living in groups. Prosociality is the term used when animals exhibit more than just sexual interactions with members of the same species. Prosociality is when societies form and relationships between individuals endure, sometimes for a lifetime. Humans and some species of monkey and apes are in this group of prosocial species.

There is an even greater level of social organisation recognised in species such as bees, where the individuals live for the greater good of the colony. Individuals of those species contribute to the group by not breeding so the queen bee can breed, or by performing specific tasks for the general functioning of the colony. Our particular kind of sociality is seen in many other mammal species and specifically in the monkeys and apes.

Scientists and philosophers mostly agree that sociality is a survival response to evolutionary pressures – a way of making a living, formulated by centuries of adaptation to the environment. There is safety in numbers if your species is prey for a large predator. Predators tend to attack individuals on the edge of the herd. For a herding animal, constantly moving from the outside to the inside of the herd minimises the chances of being on the menu of a large carnivore. Animals with higher status can sometimes be found on the inside of the herd, and lower-ranking animals on the periphery. The inside spots are safer. Perhaps you know companies like that where 'leaders' keep themselves shielded from blame or backlash? In most animal societies though, a real leader takes the lead in trying times.

Some benefits of sociality include help with the care of young born in the group, ability to gather food, and protection against predators. Disadvantages include the increased risk of disease transmission, increased competition for food and mates. The disadvantages of group living mean that there is also more chance of disagreement and conflict. That's where leadership comes in. Someone has to resolve conflict for the group. That's also where rules start to take effect. How shall we all behave if we are living together? Someone in the group has to make sure the social norms are observed and resolve conflict when they are not. On the whole, if the benefits of group living outweigh the negatives, the species is likely to be social.

Take the example of penguins. Penguins live in colonies to increase the chances of survival for both adults and their young. Among so many individuals there are more eyes to spot any predators. Sometimes penguins also work together to herd the fish they prey on. The colony of Little Penguins I looked after many years ago did breed, laying eggs, but chicks were hatched only in low numbers. Once the colony reached more than 20 birds the breeding intensity suddenly increased dramatically. The territorial displays in front of their breeding burrows became more enthusiastic and louder as the population became larger. The competition for females became more ferocious. Competition can make the entire colony more reproductively successful. Any time the colony dropped below 20 or so individuals we were back to a lower reproductive success. In this case it may have been that hearing the other males' territorial calls got all the males' hormones going. For most penguin species there are distinct advantages to living in colonies.

Humans live in small and large societies all over the world and in all manner of cultures. As a species sociality has more benefits to our survival than detriments. As much as the solitary life can sound attractive in our stressful world, few people truly live completely alone, and we are intrigued when hermits and ascetics elect to live outside society. Our species is as social as the rest of the African apes.

SOCIETY AND RECIPROCITY

Thinking about our place in the natural world is not new. Centuries ago philosophers pondered this issue. Aristotle famously quoted: 'Man is by nature a social animal.' Social animals interact highly with other animals, usually of their own species (conspecifics), to the point of having a recognisable and distinct society. Each individual in these societies has expectations of every other member of the society. Many of these rules or social norms revolve around morality. 'Do unto others as you would have them do unto you,' the Bible verse (Luke 6:31) states, and this belief has an equivalent in most other religions. The similarities between these religious rules give expression to morality in human societies *and* morality in animal societies. These rules exist in animal societies for the very same reasons. To keep the community as peaceful and harmonious as possible because living together aids survival.

Reciprocity is a significant issue in all relationships but in particular between leaders and followers, be they apes or people. It is about sharing and exchanging goods or favours and involves gratitude, memory and obligation. We often do favours for others and don't expect to be paid back immediately. The same happens when we receive favours. Perhaps weeks or months, even years later we may still feel an obligation towards the person who helped us out. My parents were born in Holland and were teenagers during the Second World War. Towards the end of the war, the people in the Netherlands suffered extreme hunger during the winter of 1944–45. Severe shortage of food and fuel led to tens of thousands of civilian deaths. In February 1945, with the help of the Swedish Red Cross, 'Swedish white bread' was distributed over the Netherlands by British and American aircraft. I was born a long time after the war and yet I heard the story many times, always told with much gratitude towards the Swedish people. Kindness and generosity remembered not only by those who received it but by their descendants seventy years later! I often wondered if the reason this event lives in the collective memory of the Dutch nation is because perhaps we feel we have not repaid the favour. As moral beings we look to repay the generosity of others.

In great ape societies sharing and doing favours serves as a model for what we too have evolved to expect as moral behaviour. The relationship between leaders and followers is one of reciprocity. There is an exchange of services for money to buy resources. Reciprocity in the workplace would be around the work performed and fair remuneration for that work. If both parties are on the same page about the quality or value of the exchange, trust starts to build. In apes this reciprocal behaviour includes anything from grooming, sex, political support, food, or even a hug after a scare.

In the Chimpanzee colony at Taronga Zoo, where I have been fortunate to watch chimps for some three decades, it is instructive to see what happens if you don't return a favour.

Spitter and Sasha, two girl chimps, get on very well and spend a lot of time together socialising and grooming. They are good friends. One day Spitter got in an altercation with a male called Shabani and Sasha did not come to help her friend. As soon as the fighting with Shabani calmed down Spitter turned on Sasha, screaming at her and hitting her. Spitter had come to Sasha's aid just a few hours earlier and expected to be recompensed during her troubles with Shabani. Sasha had to work really hard, spending time grooming and sharing food with Spitter to restore their relationship.

Our relationships at work are the same. We are happy to do favours but have innate expectations that they be repaid at some stage. This counts for leaders too. Leaders should not expect that because they are the chief this does not apply to them. From my animal experience I would suggest it applies even more to leaders than to followers. Successful chimp leaders I have known seem very aware of keeping score of whom they have done favours for. That way they know who to count on when they need political support in dominance challenges. Leaders would do well to learn from the subtleties and obligations of reciprocity we see in animal societies, to lead successfully and long term.

SOCIAL SUPPORT, BELONGING AND APPROVAL

In the workplace, thinking about and understanding belonging and reciprocity is useful. We know it matters to our cousins the Chimpanzees and Bonobos a great deal. As social animals we too crave to belong, to have the approval of our peers, our family, friends and the society we work and live in. We need to feel that the work we do is of use to our group and that we are appreciated and valued. Even if we could rightfully feel proud of our achievements, it is the approval of others that allows us to really feel good about ourselves. Animals who are bonded to others in their group are usually healthier and happier. Their immune system is likely to work well as they suffer less stress. People and animals can do amazing things when they feel secure and know they are supported by their peers and their leader.

Because of this instinctive need to belong, people generally do not want to jeopardise their position in the society they live or work in. We want to fit in and be an appreciated member of that community. Having worked with many different animals it seems to me that all social mammals have an instinctive desire to do the right thing. We use that innate desire to make our own lives and the lives of others easier. In zoos, animals are trained for procedures that will make their life better in the long run. This could be for a future dental or a medical procedure such as a vaccination. If a gorilla is trained to push his or her ear to the mesh its temperature can be taken without fuss or stress. To train animals we use a process called 'positive reinforcement'. When an animal does a desired action it is given an immediate reward. The animal will then start to link its action with the reward and over time it will start to offer that particular action on command. The urge to please is in all of us. Once we know how to get a desirable reward, we increase the frequency of the action that gets us that reward. Reward good conduct and overlook (some) bad conduct is also a people management technique in zoos. Although really bad behaviour can obviously not always be ignored or for very long!

People too generally want to do what's right and expected of them in their community or workplace. Most people will compromise to fit in to their society or clan at least to some degree. We may dress in a style that is acceptable for our workplace, we use technical jargon with our colleagues almost as a secret language and we create bonds.

Chimpanzees bond with one another through grooming sessions. We don't groom each other physically but we do 'social grooming'. Professor Robin Dunbar suggests that the human variant to physical grooming is gossip. We exchange information, secrets and 'chit-chat'. Chatting is a way of verbally grooming the other person. Chit-chat, unless it is malicious, is a way people bond with one other in the workplace.

SOCIETIES HAVE RULES AND RULES ARE ENFORCED BY LEADERS

Why should all this talk about sociality be important to us? Once a society or community forms – animal or human – there will be rules and leaders to enforce those rules. Like many primate species and other social mammals, we live in very strictly controlled societies where social norms are paramount. We need leaders to enforce these norms and more formal rules to keep our societies harmonious. The animal world gives us insights into how wild animals enforce the rules and keep the peace. For a group of animals to live together and function as a cohesive unit some individuals will come to the fore.

They make sure there *are* rules and that these are followed. How this looks depends very much on the kind of society that is formed.

How animals become the leader of their group or gain authority depends on the species. Some species will fight for the position and the strongest will win. This happens in wolves, chimps and gorillas. In some other species, such as in elephants, the leadership role might be passed down and come with age and experience, although the support of the mob can influence who becomes the leader. In some societies males dominate, in others females dominate. Other societies have a dominant pair at the helm. The next chapter illustrates some of the ways in which animals work together and make their societies operate effectively.

TOOL MAKING IN THE TARONGA ZOO CHIMPANZEES

The zookeepers thought it would be great to demonstrate the chimps' tool-using ability in front of zoo visitors. For several days their keeper, Paul Davies, gave the chimps macadamia nuts he smashed open with a rock in front of them in the night house to show them how it was done. The nuts were then given to the chimps who rather liked these novel treats.

In the animals' outdoor habitat, a solid platform was chosen and a good-sized rock was affixed to this using a chain in case the chimps hurled the rock at each other or zoo visitors. Keeper Paul threw unshelled macadamia nuts over the wet moat for the animals to open. Much to our surprise they did not run to the rock to open the nuts. They entered the night house that evening with their cheeks bulging like chipmunks. Lining up in front of Paul, they handed the nuts to their human to open. They demonstrated excellent tool use indeed: why use a rock if you can get your keeper to do it for you?

CHAPTER 2

TEAMWORK IN ANIMALS

'If you want to go fast, go alone.
If you want to go far, go together.'

AFRICAN PROVERB

Where animals or people join forces to form societies, they need to work together to achieve goals and objectives. Teamwork goes hand-in-hand with being a member of a social species. For animals teamwork is survival, literally. This chapter will look at how teamwork benefits animal societies and how it works. Animals show great teamwork and cooperation in different ways. It may enable them to hunt collectively or to more effectively defend the group against intruders. There are common elements when animals work as a team to achieve their goals, such as communication, decision making and supporting the team, and these are relevant to leaders and followers alike.

Teamwork is rooted in our long-shared history with many other mammal species. Social species are at their best when they are working collectively to overthrow an enemy or to overcome danger or threats. The role of teamwork is brilliantly illustrated in many wild animal species where the sum of the total is greater than the individual parts. For example, the Cheetah, which hunts on its own, has a low kill success rate compared with a communal pack hunter like the African Wild Dog. The ability of a group of animals or people to do things successfully depends on how well they work as a team. In animal teams each individual is trained, knows their job and the role they are to perform. There is trust amongst the team members. When our ancestors first left their forest habitat they became communal hunters. They would have had to have been very good at teamwork or we would not be here today.

A lone human hunter-gatherer on the plains of Africa would have had little defence against expert predators such as lions. As apes, our hunting techniques would have improved along with our social organisation. We didn't develop the traits of the other hunters on the plains of Africa with big teeth and claws. Instead we learned how to cooperate and work in teams to face daunting challenges.

During the last 200,000 years we have survived ice ages, famines, floods, fires, disease and other challenges. The fact that we did not become extinct during this evolutionary experiment means we got some things right, like cooperation. Looking at the number of books written on the topic of teamwork, one would think that we have forgotten how this works. Organisations use numerous consultants to run workshops on building effective teams. The industrialisation of our world, the mechanisation of jobs and the advent of the nuclear family have all taken us away from our communities. Our performance targets, job reviews and career promotions are often adversarial, pitting people against each other, which may also contribute to a society where we have to refocus on teamwork. In most cases, to get a promotion a worker has to stand out above the rest, be seen as better than the others. This may not always be compatible with the fostering of team spirit.

Fortunately both our own ancestral history and the lives of certain social animal species provide inspiring examples of how teamwork can be very successful. How animal societies are organised differs between species. However, some common traits are evident, as is the need for a leader, even in situations where all team members are clear on their roles. Different members of a team may take a leadership role on different parts of a project. Just like one lioness may be best to bring the wildebeest down while another is best at making the actual kill, with each taking a leading role where their expertise is best placed.

The following animal teams are excellent examples to show that, while leaders are important in coordinating teams, other members can contribute by taking a leading role in certain aspects of the work or decision-making.

WHITE-FACED CAPUCHIN MONKEYS – DIRECTION OF TRAVEL

In the animal world, where to go next to feed or where to sleep are essential and potentially difficult and dangerous decisions. In species with a hierarchical dominance structure it is often assumed that a single individual with high status is always be the one who makes the decisions. An interesting study by Petit and others in 2009, titled 'Collective Decision Making in White-faced Capuchin monkeys,' found that the decision to travel was not always initiated or determined by the highest-ranking animal in a group of these small South American primates.

Other animals in the group, be they male or female, would begin to move to suggest the direction of travel. When one individual monkey proposed the direction for the group to move, others could decide whether to follow or not. This allowed the whole group to take part in collective decision-making despite the fact that they had an overall leader. Close to half the group's monkeys regularly found enough followers to accompany them in the proposed direction. If they were able to recruit at least three followers, the rest of the group was likely to go along with the route suggested. Both sexes would try to recruit followers but females succeeded more frequently than males. The study found that the dominance status of the animal starting a travel movement did not seem to influence its success.

This seems to imply that even in teams with a hierarchical structure, lower ranking team members can make important suggestions. The success of those suggestions is determined by the amount of support an individual receives from the team members.

What can we learn from White-faced Capuchin monkeys about teamwork?
• Not all ideas have to be initiated by the leader.
• Team members should be encouraged to share the burden of decision making.

AFRICAN WILD DOGS – SNEEZING TO VOTE

The African Wild Dog is not the strongest or the fastest predator in its habitat. Their fabulous teamwork however makes them, on average, more successful than any other predator in the same environment. The Leopard hunts alone and has an average success rate of 10 per cent. The Lion only has a success rate of 17 per cent when hunting alone, but when a group of Lions hunts together this increases to 30 per cent. The Cheetah, the world's fastest animal on land, works alone and makes a kill in 50 per cent of its attempts. The African Wild Dog learns from generation to generation how to hunt as a team. More than 80 per cent of their attacks end in a kill. Speed and size alone don't always deliver a good result; cooperation does. African Wild Dogs, when they work as a team, are so much better than their individual efforts.

Wild dogs live in complex hierarchies in which usually only the alpha male and alpha female breed. Pack members regurgitate food for the young but they will also share food with other adults who haven't come on the hunt. They are not usually aggressive with each other and don't fight over food. Instead they beg from other adults to let them know they are hungry. Adults will also allow younger animals to eat their fill before eating themselves.

Jordan Michelmore, who cares for African Wild Dogs in Taronga Western Plains Zoo in Dubbo, Australia, describes how these dogs look out for one another:

'The last litter of African Wild Dog pups started coming out of the den at about five or six weeks old. We feed the whole pack together on a big carcass. When the pups come to feed, all the adult dogs stand back from the food. Only once the pups have had their fill do the adult dogs approach the food and eat themselves. If a pup has not had enough to eat it goes up to any adult and starts making this high-pitched squeal. If the adult has food in their mouth they just drop it. If they have already eaten they will regurgitate for the pup. One of my favourite things to watch!'

Recently it was discovered that African Wild Dogs sneeze to vote for hunting decisions. Wild dogs do what is called a 'rally'. They run around, and try to rouse the others into action. Sometimes the rally will end with the dogs going off to hunt, sometimes they will just lie down again and sleep or rest. Researchers noticed that there was, at times, a lot of sneezing going on. One of the researchers, Neil Jordan, relates that when there was more sneezing at the rally, the dogs were more likely to start the hunt. This led him to believe that in African Wild Dogs, sneezes may 'function as a voting mechanism to establish group consensus.' Neil Jordan, now at Taronga Western Plains Zoo, explains:

'The important decisions in the pack are about when and where to go hunting. There are a number of different drivers within the pack as to the best time and the best place to go. Knowing the place is probably based on experience, while deciding when to go is probably based on individual hunger level. If only a few animals are very hungry while the others are very sated, then there can be some conflict on making that collective decision.'

Neil observed that African Wild Dog packs spent most of the

day in the shade after hunting, to digest and rest, until a rally started:

'The rally is a very excitable social behaviour. Usually one individual starts the process; not always the same one. They put their ears back and go into this stalking posture, attempting to rouse the others. When the others join in, there's lots of vocalising; lots of twittering, unusual in canids as it sounds like a kind of bird call. Lots of ritual parallel running and greeting each other. It can look like organised chaos. They also do lots of scent-marking at this time, and immediately following the rally you can hear these sorts of 'sneezes'. They stand still and rapidly expel air, apparently voluntarily, through their noses. I got the impression that something was going on with this behaviour, and by observing the pack I felt that I could pretty accurately predict if they were going to move off or just rest again, based purely (I thought) on the number of sneezes.

As I got pretty good at predicting I realised I was basing that on the sneezing. So we started collecting data to see if that was a useful signal to predict if the dogs would make a move to hunt. It seems like it was, and the number of sneezes in particular was quite important. We classified rallies into two different types: rallies with an alpha involved, and rallies where the alphas just remained resting. We found that if the alpha was involved there were fewer sneezes before the pack moved off. A stronger vote appeared to come from at least one of the dominant dogs. If alphas decided they wanted to go, the pack generally dutifully followed. If the alpha was reluctant then high levels of sneezing from the rest of the pack could be sufficient to convince the leaders to lead. Once the decision was made, and regardless of their initial enthusiasm for the move, one of the dominant pair was often at the front when the pack moved away. Obviously we don't know what's going in their heads but it seems that the dominant animals are coerced when the rest of the pack is keen to go. In fact, when there are 10 or more sneezes the dominant dogs are coerced into getting a move on.'

Although the vote may not be entirely democratic, giving only the alphas extra voting power, it is not dissimilar to the Chair of the Board having a 'casting vote'. If a dominant dog starts the rally it takes only three sneezes for the pack to initiate the hunt. If the alpha animals don't really want to go they do take the majority vote to heart and lead the hunt. The pack communicates during the rally and the hunt with calls and body postures respectively, and so clearly there is more to discover on how leadership works in this species.

African Wild Dogs are loyal creatures. Each member in the pack will protect other members in critical situations. Whether sharing food, or protecting and teaching the pups, wild dogs commit themselves to the pack. For a team in the workplace loyalty is equally important. Working together on assignments a team would do well look to African Wild Dogs for examples of decision making and supporting the pack.

What can we learn from African Wild Dogs about teamwork?
• Good teamwork can be more successful than speed or strength.

- Loyalty to the pack adds to effectiveness and helps a team thrive when competition in the field is fierce.
- Leaders can successfully accept team input.

MEERKATS – LOOKING OUT FOR ONE ANOTHER

Meerkats have a survival strategy based on mutual trust and cooperation. They are social animals living in groups of five to forty animals in large underground networks with multiple entrances which they only leave during the day. Their society is matriarchal and mother is definitely in charge. Although males can have dominance battles, female Meerkats have much higher levels of aggression than males. They invest a lot in producing young but the right to breed and succeed is worth the effort. Most Meerkats within the same mob are siblings and offspring of the alpha pair. As with African Wild Dogs, there is a strong hierarchy in Meerkats and only the alpha male and alpha female get to breed. The dominant female leads the group to forage, decides which direction they travel and which sleeping burrow to occupy. Louise Ginman has cared for small and large carnivores for more than two decades at Taronga Zoo. During this time she has seen several leadership changes in the Meerkat colony.

'I have seen some great Meerkat leaders in our group over the years. Namibia was the first female leader I looked after. She came from a group of four sisters: Namibia, Botswana, Kalahari and Victoria. Namibia stood out very early on as a leader. She was tough and kept her sisters in line. Hard on them to a certain point, she let them know she was always in charge. But as soon as they accepted her leadership, she let them be. Namibia was an exceptional leader and was well respected. This respect showed when she became really old and her breeding male died. She was not ousted from the group. The group allowed her to stay, albeit at a lower rank. She lived out her days in her family, even though the hierarchy had shifted to a new leader.'

Despite the obvious dominance of the alpha pair, all team members take responsibility for the security of the mob. Where teamwork is strong in this species is in the role of the 'sentinel', most often performed by a helper, or a non-breeder. The sentinel is the lookout, watching for possible predators and other potential threats to the community any time the gang is foraging.

The sentinel role is shared around all gang members, even the alpha pair. This altruism helps family members to survive. Meerkats place a lot of trust in their sentinels to ensure the entire group is safe. When on guard duty, Meerkats will regularly give a call known as the 'watchman's song', just to let the others know there is a sentinel watching out for them. When a predator is spotted, the Meerkat on sentry will give a warning bark. All other members of the gang will run and hide in one of the many bolt holes they have spread across their territory. In his book *Meerkat Manor*, Tim Clutton-Brock describes how Meerkats have distinct categories of alarm calls: a call for aerial predators, one for terrestrial predators and yet another for snakes.

Each of these calls has an urgency pitch, which generates a different response. The high-urgency calls have the fastest response rate, with the entire group running to the nearest burrow. The sentinel will be barking to keep the others underground. If there is no threat, the sentry Meerkat will stop barking and the mob will be safe to emerge. Other calls are not so urgent.

Louise Ginman recently saw lots of wild Meerkat groups close up in South Africa and commented on her observations of the alpha female and the sentinels in the mob:

'The head female will often be the first to pop her head out of the burrow in the morning and make sure the coast is clear. If there is no danger, the rest of the family will emerge from the burrow and start to sun themselves. The matriarch leads that family to forage. It is her knowledge of the landscape that leads the mob to where the food is, where the water is, where all the burrow systems are. At the end of every foraging day they have to end up in a burrow. If they don't they are in big trouble. Once darkness falls many predators come out. What the group gets from their leader is the fact that they guide to seasonal food sources and to water. As a desert species they don't need a lot of water, but it's good to know where it is. Equally, if they don't get led to a burrow at night they could be in real danger. The matriarch has the skills and knowledge that the mob needs to survive. The rest of the mob follows and supports their leader. She is the only one to breed. The breeding female works with the breeding male to defend the territory. Meerkats tend to perform a lot of sentry duty in situations where predation risk is higher. Meerkats that volunteer for sentry duty are the most satiated. The breeding pair do sentry duty as well, and if they see nobody is watching they too will stand guard. They are always making sure that the family can forage safely.'

Meerkats will also babysit any young in the group. Older female babysitters will often even lactate to feed the alpha pair's young while the dominant female is foraging with the rest of the group. They will protect the young from any threat, often endangering their own lives to do so. On warning of a danger, the babysitter will take the young underground to safety or collect all the young together and lie on top of them if retreating underground is not possible. Whilst the leaders are busy producing the next generation, the rest of the Meerkat team makes sure that safety from predators is a top priority. It takes a village to raise a Meerkat!

What can we learn from Meerkats about teamwork?
• Meerkats take responsibility and do the job that needs doing.
• Meerkats place trust in the members of their team.
• Good communication is key to success.

HONEY BEES – COMMUNICATION

Honey Bees work together and show leadership at the same time. A single colony can house up to 30,000 insects. Each bee has a very specific role in the community. Hives are like large well-run organisations. Some bees are destined to breed, others maintain the hive or process the collected nectar. Collecting nectar for the hive is a significant job and involves many individuals. Although technically the queen bee is the leader, it appears that she does not lead anything at all other than egg production and determining the eventual gender of each of her eggs. As the eggs move from her ovaries to oviducts she decides whether each one is to be fertilised or not. If an egg is fertilised, it will become a worker or queen bee. If it is not fertilised, it will become a drone. Each group of bees collectively takes charge of their specific responsibilities.

So how do you quickly recruit a good number of fellow nectar foragers for the hive when you're a bee? The nectar may only be available for a short time and needs to be gathered fast. Scout bees go out to see what they can find and if they come back engorged from a good source they need to let the other bees know. Bees can communicate with precision the exact location of the sweet nectar. When the scout returns to the hive she first offloads and distributes the nectar to the receiver bees in the hive. She then begins to dance. There are two types of dances: the so-called round dance and the waggle dance.

Bees dancing in front of the hive have been described and commented on for many centuries. The Austrian Nobel laureate Karl von Frisch was one of the first to document the meaning of the waggle dance. He himself doubted at first that a creature so small could do something so smart. The waggle dance, performed in a figure of eight, specifies the exact location of flowers that are more than 100m (330ft) away. It gives information about the direction and the exact distance of the food source. The dancing is more enthusiastic and goes on for longer the more abundant the source is. If the bounty is not too excellent the dance will be shorter and less energetic. It will also recruit less new foragers.

The round dance, on the other hand, is performed for closer nectar sources that are within 25–100m (80–330ft). The returning bee gives away some more nectar and repeats the dance some three times. The round dance does not tell the bees about the direction of the flowers. Instead recruited bees use olfactory information from the dancer. The bees can recognise the fragrance of the flowers on the dancing bee and they can smell the dancing bee's scent on the flowers.

Similar dances are used to help swarming bees find a new home. In this case the scouts dance to guide the swarm into a hollow tree or another suitable site. Once the bees have inspected various potential hive sites the vote is taken. To vote for a site the bees dance in front of it and the site with the most dancers will be selected.

Bees will defend the hive by stinging any intruder. When a Honey Bee stings a human it can't pull the barbed stinger back out. By leaving the stinger behind it also leaves a part of its abdomen, digestive tract, muscles and nerves behind. This means the animal dies defending the hive – the ultimate sacrifice for the greater good of the team!

What can we learn from Honey Bees about teamwork?
• Sharing information accurately and precisely helps the team to work efficiently.
• Each scout is *both* a leader *and* a team player.
• Voting for decisions by team members maintains cooperation.
• Absolute loyalty to the team brings big dividends for everyone.

WHAT'S COMMON IN ANIMAL TEAMWORK?
Every animal society finds unique solutions to the specific ways they have to work together to eke out a living. Even in very hierarchal

animal societies like African Wild Dogs or Meerkats there is room for individuals to come together as a team. Each team member contributes to the society's success. There are common elements that make animal teams work, namely the need to work out what the goals of the group are, who is in the team, how the team bonds and develops trust, how to communicate, how decisions are made, how new team members are trained and the role of each team member.

WHAT ARE THE GOALS OF THE GROUP?

What would the goals of a troop of gorillas be? They want to find food and water, to make babies, have shelter, and deter any enemies or predators. Easy! Human beings have many more options when selecting our collective team goals. The leader has an important role to play in working with the team to jointly agree on the goals but they need to be as clear as the goals of a troop of gorillas. Given that we can communicate concepts and beliefs very effectively, we are certainly capable of clearly articulating and sharing our goals. Humans have the evolutionary attributes for collaboration and we can cooperate when it really matters. We do, however, need to make sure that the collective goal is always clear to the whole team. The role of the team leader is also to make sure that the goal is understandable, achievable, that the team has the resources to complete it and, above all, it has merit.

Simon Sinek, in his book *Start With Why*, makes a compelling argument for organisations and individuals to ask the question: '*Why* are we doing this?' What is the purpose of the organisation or the team? Over and above making money, is this part of a greater good? Wild animals are very clear about their raison d'etre. Just like the goals of the gorilla troop, we should be clear about why we do what we do. Teams, be they animal or human, need to know their raison d'etre.

WHO IS IN 'THE TEAM?'

Most animals will cooperate really well with their direct kin but not so well with any individuals outside their immediate community. In ancient times, we also teamed up mostly with family or our clan, but in contrast to many animal species we do have the ability to work well with individuals beyond our tribe.

Teams work best if we feel kinship with the team members. As a species, we can be influenced into feeling we are more related to others than we actually are through common goals and beliefs rather than blood ties. If we believe in the same things we can adopt each other as 'kin'. In contrast to animals, our communication skills are so advanced we can share complicated concepts and ideas with words and gestures in such ways that others can understand them. If we believe in the same things, we can create short- and longer-term kin-like alliances with relative strangers to become a team. The leader is essential in making people feel part of the team, fostering the feeling of belonging, of being kin, among the members. Leaders can do this by including the team in planning, for example, or by sharing responsibility for decisions and by celebrating even small successes.

HOW DO TEAMS BOND AND DEVELOP TRUST?

Ape societies keep their alliances in working order by spending time together. They sit together and they groom each other. This maintains and strengthens their bonds. The human alternative to grooming is spending time together and talking. To mention Professor Dunbar's book *Grooming, Gossip and the Evolution of Language* again; gossip is at its basic level an *exchange of information*. Thousands of years ago this would have been fundamental to our survival, appraising each other about where the lions were last seen, or where the wildebeest could be hunted, for example.

Gossip continues to perform an essential social service. Dunbar defines gossip as 'social chit-chat'. Our species is good at vocalising and we use our ability to communicate as an alternative to grooming. People chat to create and maintain allegiances with other people. Matthew Fienberg, a Stanford University researcher, states that 'Groups that allow their members to gossip sustain cooperation and deter selfishness better than those that don't'. Research shows that social chit-chat not only creates and maintains bonds but it keeps us in line. Our reputations could be damaged if we get caught out not being entirely honest or do not reciprocate the favours we have received. This helps to keep our societies cooperating with each other in the same way animal communities maintain their cohesion.

Animal teams learn to trust each other by doing things together and relying on each other to succeed. If the foraging Meerkats can't rely on the individual on guard duty, family members may be killed by predators. If the Honey Bees can't rely on their hive mates to bring back the right information about where the food sources are, the hive may fail and disband. In our workplaces, the exchange of information may not be a matter of life or death, but we too have an innate need to trust our teammates. Trust in the contributions of members in animal teams builds as they prove themselves trustworthy.

Many species like Chimpanzees, Meerkats and African Wild Dogs have elaborate greeting rituals when they meet up after even a short absence. This helps to reaffirm the ties and trust between the individuals. In our workplaces too, the way we acknowledge and greet one another, when we arrive at work in the morning, or after the weekend or a vacation, probably serves a similar purpose. With a greeting we say, 'You matter to me'. In different human cultures the greeting rituals vary, but all serve the purpose of acknowledging the other person and showing respect. A greeting is the start of a relationship upon which we can build trust or reaffirm an existing relationship. Leaders set an example each and every day by acknowledging the team when they arrive in the morning and saying goodbye when they leave. A leader who sneaks in and out of their office without greetings neither makes people feel valued and worthy, nor inspires others to trust them. All social animal groups have elaborate greetings to reaffirm the bonds of trust.

BIOLOGY AND CULTURE

One definition of culture is *the ideas, customs and social behaviour of a particular people or society*. Primatologists increasingly speak of 'culture' to explain observations of wild primates. In wild Chimpanzees, there are different ways tools are used in different groups. In Japanese Macaques, a culture of washing potatoes developed and slowly spread through the entire community. In the early 1950s a group of researchers saw one young female Japanese Macaque dip a potato in a river, presumably to wash the sand off it. Until that time the other monkeys had only brushed the sand off with their hands. The culture of washing the potatoes in the river was soon copied and within a decade all the macaques on the island were washing their potatoes.

Biology and culture both influence how we and other animals live our lives. Biology is the hardwiring we brought with us from our ancient ancestors. Culture is more about 'how we do things around here'. The two go alongside each other and can't always be pulled apart easily. Underlying the diverse cultures in people around the world is that same biology that shapes our emotions and a great deal of our conduct. Culture has developed in parallel to our biology and influences our lives in similar ways. Culture can adapt to a new situation much faster than our genes can.

COMMUNICATION

Animal teams have found different and innovative ways of exchanging information. We have seen that Honey Bees dance, African Wild Dogs sneeze, and Meerkats use different alarm calls for different types of predators. Animals grunt, hoot, screech, growl, mew, roar, trumpet, snort, purr, hiss and make many more communication sounds. Apes, in particular, also use gestures and facial expressions and many other animals use body postures to convey meanings to others in their team. We too have an array of options to communicate.

We humans can use our voice, gestures, postures and facial expressions. Just like our animal cousins, humans will often have an instant opinion about a person, what they said or did. You can't make a good first impression twice so it's important to carefully plan how to best communicate the true meaning of what you want to share. In animal teams posture, body language and facial expressions all influence how an individual is received. For us, over and above our words, these postures, gestures and facial expressions affect how others 'hear' what we say.

DECISION MAKING

An example of a democratic approach to decision making in teams is epitomised by the African Wild Dog and its 'sneezing vote'. The White-faced Capuchin monkey also shows that members of the group other than the alpha male can make suggestions about where to go next if enough group support is evident. The ability to take part in decision making is inherent in many animal societies and appropriate in human organisations. The team leader needs to create a culture that allows for the free flow of ideas, a safe space to have wild ideas, if you like, and where opinions are shared respectfully. Leaders influence how the team makes decisions. A leader showcasing respect for the ideas of others and supporting democratic decision-making influences the team culture in a positive way. Shared decision making allows for more creativity. 'Many heads are better than one' can lead to more individual investment in projects and more job satisfaction. A leader who allows people to contribute and feel valued for their input creates longevity for the team.

LEARNING ON THE JOB AND THE ROLE OF EACH TEAM MEMBER

Animals learn on the job how to fit in with the team. Young chimps, for example, need to learn the rules of their society. They have a small tuft of white hair on their bottom where a tail once would have been. This disappears by about the age of five. Until that time they are easily forgiven most social misdemeanours such as hitting the dominant male or jumping on an adult. Once they lose that white tuft they are expected to know the rules. The white tuft is like driving with 'learner plates' on your car!

Animal teams are forgiving towards new or young members still learning their role or how society works. Young Lions for example will go out with the pride to make a kill but the more experienced adults will lead the hunt. For the young Lions it's a combination of observation and practice whilst experienced adults supervise and lend a helping hand when needed. Animal leaders give team members opportunities to learn the job over time and step in to help out when needed.

When Meerkats take their turn at guarding whilst the mob is foraging, or when Lions take their place in the hunt, each team member knows what is expected of them to help achieve the group's goal. Some lionesses will be better at taking down a gazelle than others in the group, but each member contributes the very best of their skills. Animal teams exemplify how the coordination of teamwork does not necessarily come from the highest-ranking individual or the oldest member in the team. Despite that, the team leader ultimately influences that positive culture in the group.

REALLY WORKING TOGETHER

Examples from the animal world clearly demonstrate that working together allows social animal communities to survive and thrive. Humans have even more useful attributes that enhance teamwork. Our language abilities help significantly with coordination and sharing the vision and goals of the team. We are the species that has the ability for unparalleled cooperation. We can work with unrelated, unknown strangers in times of trouble such as natural disaster recovery after tsunamis or earthquakes. We work in international teams doing important cancer research with people from different, far away organisations contributing to the outcomes. We develop treaties between countries to safeguard the passage of migratory birds or to protect our natural heritage for the global community.

Animals give the best of themselves to contribute to their teams and role-model the attributes we value most in our teams. Good teamwork may look like it just happens, but it is the result of good leadership. Although Meerkats are known for their teamwork, the role of leader is crucial in keeping their society working well together. Louise Ginman comments on the role of the matriarch in Meerkat society:

'To be a head female you may have to fight your way to the top. If it is not actual fighting there is a lot of jostling and posturing. The establishment of hierarchy in Meerkats starts from a very young age with squabbling over food and establishing their rank in the hierarchy. It's a linear hierarchy, but it is fluid and can change if an animal is not well, for example, or comes into season. There is a female and a male linear hierarchy. Generally females don't get too involved in male squabbles and males don't get involved in female squabbles. As the hierarchy develops very early in life, an individual who is able to maintain their high rank when they grow up they can become the head female.

Nairobi was another great Meerkat leader I have worked with. She was Namibia's granddaughter and had very good genes, perhaps inheriting some of the leadership characteristics of her grandmother. She did have fights with other members of the group to establish her dominance, but very few. That's the thing with good animal leaders, they don't have to fight as much as some of the more insecure individuals have to. Insecure Meerkat leaders will fight a lot to keep their dominance over the others. They are also more likely to bite the tails of the others to get them to leave the group. They seem too insecure in their leadership to allow a challenging group member to stay. Nairobi, though, only enforced as much as she needed to maintain the harmony of the group. No more, no less. She still is a confident leader. That confidence gives other Meerkats the confidence in her as the leader and they are willing to support her.'

For an animal team to work at peak performance the following has to happen:
- The leader has to be trusted by the team as the right one to lead them to success.
- The leader has to spend time building cohesion in the team.
- The leader has to create a sense of identity for the team, clarifying purpose and values.

The examples in this chapter show that individual animals take on leadership tasks from time to time, even though the leader guides the identity and goals for the team. Great animal leaders monitor performance but don't micromanage. They empower the team, share responsibility and ensure team accountability for the results.

CHAPTER 3

A NATURAL HISTORY OF LEADERSHIP

'You can take the ape out of the jungle,
but not the jungle out of the ape.'

FRANS DE WAAL

Much has changed in the world since our apish beginnings but these changes are mostly cultural, not biological. Our brains have not changed at the same speed as our circumstances. Our evolution has shaped us to expect the same leadership qualities we valued in ancient times. In our ancient past leadership aided the greater good of the community and followers were closely involved in selecting their leaders. Our leadership culture has changed but our expectations of leadership have not. The lifestyle of early humans has many similarities with semi-nomadic, group-living mammals and primates in particular. It is reasonable to assume therefore that we have faced the same dilemmas and have consequently developed a unique but comparable leadership model – most likely based on our last common ancestor that we shared with Bonobos and Chimpanzees. However, our innate way of interacting with the world may, in fact, go back even further with an ancient mammalian ancestor.

What are the implications of this mismatch of culture and biology? How can leaders overcome these challenges? In this chapter I hope to have readers think about leadership in a different way. Normally leadership is viewed from the perspective of the person who runs the show. Yet, a lot of leadership styles in wild animals are as much about the followers as they are about the leader. Looking at leadership also from the perspective of followers gives a different view of the requirements of a good leader.

This chapter also examines the discrepancies between our ancient environments and our modern environments. We are facing the challenges of massive changes in our circumstances with the same body and the same brain that served us well a couple of hundred thousand years ago. Leadership in our human ancestors was often related to physical prowess, such as the ability to hunt or to fight strangers. The leader would have been selected for the task at hand and supported by the group as the right one for the job. Followers would have been as closely involved in the selection of the leader as our primate relatives often are.

WHY IS OUR EVOLUTION RELEVANT?

Unless you are a biologist or a scientist you probably don't think about evolution every day and with everything you see and do.

I do.

I can't help it.

Evolution is all around me and influences how I think about the world. Spending decades observing animals will do that to you perhaps. Everything alive today has physical and behavioural characteristics that have been passed down through the generations. Our evolution is what has shaped our feelings about how leaders act and what followers want from their leaders.

The principle of evolution in a species is basically about keeping good traits and getting rid of bad ones. If the species keeps negative qualities and gets rid of the characteristics that are beneficial it will become extinct. Natural selection is about adapting to the circumstances you find yourself in. If the circumstances change faster than the evolutionary process can keep up then we can find ourselves with features that were useful once upon a time for challenges we no longer face, while not being very well adapted to the new challenges.

There are plenty examples in nature where a species is in the process of major evolutionary change. The Giant Panda is a good example. It is classified as a bear. It still has a carnivore gut but eats mostly bamboo. Some of its dentition has changed to cope with all that chewing of vegetation and it has a forefoot adaptation for grasping bamboo stems. The panda gut, however, is still poorly adapted to breaking down bamboo because it is deficient in cellulose-digesting enzymes. So the panda needs to eat enormous amounts of bamboo in order to get enough nutrition from its now 'favourite' food. Evolutionary adaptations to new circumstances take a very long time to complete.

Like the Giant Panda, humans too can be considered to be mismatched to our current situation because of the very fast changes to our social and cultural environment. We did a lot of adapting to suit our nomadic lifestyle and later to suit our lives as hunter-gatherers before we became sedentary farmers about 10,000 years ago. If we consider a generation to be around 20 years, this means there have only been 500 generations since we settled down to farming – not a long time at all in evolutionary terms. Not enough time to make changes both to our biology, brain and behaviour to suit the world we now live in.

Fossil evidence shows that our brain size has been very stable for the last 200,000 years. Evolutionary psychologists Tooby and Cosmides assert that *'our modern skulls house a Stone-Age mind'*. The process that makes relatively simple changes to our brain can take many thousands of years. We have not had those thousands of years to make the changes to our brain that would match all the challenges of our current circumstances. Our prehistoric past is important in understanding the evolved mechanisms that underpin leadership and followership.

ARE WE MISMATCHED WITH TODAY'S WORLD?

The Mismatch Theory is about the conflict between our biology and our culture. This concept in evolutionary biology suggests that the traits evolved to be beneficial to our species became less useful once major changes in our environment happened. This happens in humans and animals when there is rapid environmental change. There is a big difference in how we lived in the first millions of years of our history compared with how we lived as hunter-gatherers, and compared again to the very recent change to an agricultural society. This move to agriculture and a sedentary lifestyle happened only around ten to twelve thousand years ago, and even less in some societies. The implication of this suggests that we may not be perfectly matched with the circumstances we find ourselves in now.

In ancient times, leadership revolved around major problems of survival and day-to-day decisions about group movement. Our leadership styles evolved when people lived in small, largely kin-based clans. Leadership was likely informal and fairly egalitarian. This ancient leadership style may still influence the way we respond to leaders today.

Understanding how wild animals organise their societies, their leadership and followership may give us an insight into what our ancient selves evolved to expect from *our* leaders. If we compare leadership in animals and leadership in people, our leadership style today may be misguided. When you observe how much of the leadership in wild animals is about the followers it allows for a different view. Our ancient leadership styles were likely to be very similar to what we still see in the leadership of other mammals, the great apes in particular.

Dissatisfaction with leaders can be a big problem for organisations. The mismatch between expectations and reality may be the reason that up to 60 to 70 per cent of employees report that the most stressful part of their job is dealing with their immediate supervisor. What leaders want and what followers expect does not always correlate. Our expectations of leaders are likely to be hardwired. From our ancient past to the present day, the world has changed but our feelings have not.

When great apes influence the selection of their leader it is likely to be a leader with positive leadership qualities. As mammals we are designed for caring and compassion. Mammals like us have extended maternal care. With maternal care comes the ability to bond. This bonding gives mammals the prerequisite model for all other attachments including leadership. Bonding is crucial to our species and many other social species. As species, the African great apes and humans alike are gregarious by nature, not by choice. It is a biological need. How we feel about leadership also goes back to prehuman times. This may be the root cause of a mismatch between the expectations of leaders and followers in our modern world.

WHAT IS EVOLUTIONARY LEADERSHIP THEORY?

Evolutionary Leadership Theory looks at leadership from an evolutionary perspective. Evolutionary psychology proposes that our thoughts, feelings and actions are the product of innate psychological processes. These processes have evolved to help people to effectively deal with situations that influence survival and reproduction. Evolutionary theory proposes that both leadership and followership were important at one time for the survival and reproductive success of our ancestors.

As we started to live in larger more socially complex communities some 200,000 years ago, conflicts within the community and with strangers would have become more frequent as the population grew and competition became more prevalent. Leaders were needed to either resolve any conflict or to fight invaders at the border.

Evolutionary Leadership Theory was introduced by Mark van Vugt, Professor of Evolutionary Psychology at VU University Amsterdam in the Netherlands, who defines leadership as 'the result of a Darwinian process of evolution via natural selection whereby groups of animals, be it mammals, insects, birds or fish, that form effective leader-follower relations, do better than groups that fail to coordinate around a leader.' If we take that evolutionary approach to looking at leadership it is obvious why we see so many parallels in the animal world.

It is of course impossible to directly study our ancient forebears for the way that they managed leadership and followership behaviours. Fortunately leaders and followers have developed in all social animal groups and these observable animal models illustrate how we too were influenced by the same pressures to develop leader-follower relations. Leadership is thought to have evolved in response to the need for group coordination. As we saw in the previous chapter, a classic example of this can be seen in the decision-making of capuchin monkeys about travel movements. Being social is closely related to protection from predators, so social animals have a better chance of survival if they move together. But how is the decision to move made? Who gets the final say? Different species have come up with different solutions to this dilemma. From Lions to baboons, gorillas to African Wild Dogs, social mammals have cultivated a leadership model to deal with these questions. African Elephants, for instance, have developed a leadership style that values 'corporate' history. Old females are the leaders in these matriarchal societies because they hold indispensable knowledge in a changeable climate, like leading the herd to a waterhole only she can remember.

Evolutionary theory is both used effectively and abused by some people who use it to justify why we are an inherently aggressive species. Darwin never intended his theory of natural selection to mean that we can ruthlessly compete with others. Natural selection shaped us to be cooperative and we have inhibitions against acts that can harm the survival of our group. We too have probably evolved to be suspicious of strangers until they are strangers no longer. Darwin did believe that both animals and humans are capable of kindness. He was right about so many things, he is probably correct in this too. Our competitiveness does not make us more human, it may make us inhumane. Our natural inclination for kindness also influences how we think about the positive effect that good leaders can have.

The Evolutionary Leadership Theory offers a fresh perspective on why leadership is challenging. Understanding the evolved mechanisms influencing leadership shows that good leaders have an accurate idea of their own intentions and how followers react to their leadership style. We expect leaders to take care of their people. Whereas most managers understand that pleasing their superiors leads to greater career progression than pleasing subordinates. That too is a mismatch of expectations.

IMPLICATIONS OF EVOLUTIONARY LEADERSHIP

So far, *Homo sapiens* have spent about 99 per cent of their evolutionary history in small kinship groups. Just like our primate cousins in Africa. Evolution is a slow process and we are probably only in the process *now* of selecting for adaptations that help us thrive in today's society. In the meantime, our bodies and brains continue to reflect the humans we were in our ancient history.

The discrepancy between our ancient environments and our modern environments is enormous. In the long-distant past people knew their leader personally. They would have known what the leader 'stood for', their values and their ethos. Leaders today, both in the workplace or in politics, are often not known personally to the people they lead. In the case of politicians, we would like to know their personal values but we mostly only know the values of the party, not the person. We have a deep-seated need to know our leaders on a personal level but the modern business world often makes that unachievable. This explains why employees are often heard to speak disparagingly of decisions made by 'head-office' – remote decision making, by people unknown.

Our evolutionary history saw us living in small, relatively egalitarian communities for millions of years and this still influences how we respond to leadership today. If the boss's leadership does not correlate with the qualities that were important to us in ancient times, this may lead to efforts to overthrow the leader, to change jobs or to change careers. Our ancient societies had networks with a maximum of some 150 individuals. Chimpanzees gather in groups of up to 100 animals, whereas Bonobos reportedly sometimes have gatherings of between 150 and 200 individuals. These are the numbers that researcher Professor Robin Dunbar believes humans can hold together cohesively without forceful control.

Group size is a crucial consideration when we design zoo enclosures. We always look to the natural history of the species to determine the most suitable group size and composition, knowing that this in itself will make the animals feel more relaxed and at home. This provides the best opportunity for the group to be cohesive and harmonious. The same approach is needed when managing human groups in the workplace.

Human leadership style can be adjusted to minimise the implications of Evolutionary Leadership Theory. For example, the leadership team can replicate natural team sizes and organisational structures. Dunbar uses examples from medieval villages to military companies to emphasise that around 150 people is the optimum number for a group to bond and function as a community. Keeping work teams to this village-sized number provides people with a sense of belonging in their workplace. The Gore-Tex company has taken this optimal number of staff to heart and in each factory they limit the number of employees to 150 so that 'everyone knows everyone'. Additionally, the leaders of such a clan-sized group can know all the staff by name, know the work they do and value them as individuals. Thus creating an environment that feels like a community and developing a culture that brings harmony. Consideration of these basic human preferences to know leaders personally and understand their values, and to limit the size and location of the team, can make a big difference to how followers feel about the leader. Paying attention to the natural dispositions of our wilder selves can encourage bonding, group cohesion and therefore productivity.

THE DARWIN AWARDS

The Darwin Awards are awarded annually to honour Charles Darwin, the father of evolution. The awards commemorate individuals who, through their noble idiocy, make the ultimate sacrifice of their own lives, to improve our species' chance of long-term survival. In other words, they are cautionary tales about people who kill themselves in really stupid ways, thus eliminating themselves from the human race and not passing on their defective genes to future generations, thereby significantly improving the gene pool for posterity.

A 2018 Darwin Award winner was Zaim Khalis. On 28th January 2018, in Selangor, Malaysia, Zaim spotted a 3.7m (12ft) Reticulated Python sleeping on the side of the road. 'That is worth money!' thought Zaim. The 35-year-old prepared to catch the snake with gloves and a sickle. Zaim held the reptile's head high as he transported it home by motorbike. Swinging in the air, the displeased snake wrapped its body round and round its captor, constricting him. Zaim swerved off the road and was found by passers-by the next morning. A post-mortem confirmed his death by strangulation. Zaim Khalis was described as a quiet person who kept to himself.

Evolution, through natural selection, is a harsh mistress.

HIERARCHY AND DOMINANCE

Leadership and hierarchy are closely connected. Our tendency to form hierarchies was formed way back in our primate evolution. All of the African great apes live in highly hierarchical societies. High-ranking males and females are more successful in having more offspring that survive. Those at the bottom of the hierarchy don't do as well. That's motivation for moving up the hierarchy, posturing for position, for improving one's status. This affirmation of rank still has its effects in our modern societies. From hierarchies we develop leaders and followers.

What do primate leaders do? They coordinate group movement, resolve conflict in the group, they punish wayward members and, if they are good, they foster group cohesion. They also protect the group from invasions. Ape leaders have a role in sharing resources, food in particular, and consoling distressed members of the community. Some primate leaders are very dominant, others less so. Hierarchy resulting in dominance is also a part of our primate history. All our closely related primate cousins live in societies that are typified by hierarchies and dominance. Humans evolved with similar power structures and modern humans continue to demonstrate this propensity. Social dominance is always on our mind, consciously or unconsciously, from the depth of the bowing in Japan to the class-associated accents in the United Kingdom.

Hierarchies and dominance, for a leader, are easier strategies to manipulate than demonstrating true leadership by modelling conduct that inspires followers. Although an animal reaches the alpha position often through contest, once the relative positions are established the situation can be quite stable. The need for further contest has been removed – at least for a while. Even animals lower on the ladder are often happy, for now, with the tension dissipated and calm returned. Hierarchies are formed by us too, even when they really don't matter much. Having been one myself (a long time ago), I am always amused by teenage girls. Often grouping in threes, it is almost immediately obvious who the alpha of the trio is. She sets the dress code and pulls it off best, while the other two imitate the style in as much detail as possible, without wearing the exact same thing. The alpha's posture, confidence and the way the other two behave around her all make the pecking order clear to them and to any observers.

Every society, be they animal or human, has evolved a leadership system to suit specific circumstances. In our modern world, businesses are essentially dominance hierarchies where high-ranking individuals make the decisions often with little influence from the followers. Hierarchies help to bring order to complex animal societies, but dominance is sometimes a default position for some leaders. Successful animal leaders, on the other hand, only use as much dominance as they need for the circumstances – no more, no less.

OUR INSTINCTS RULE

Acknowledging our instincts has significant implications for leaders. The *Cambridge Dictionary* defines instinct as: 'the way people or animals naturally react or behave, without having to think or learn about it.' It is still popular to think that animals are ruled by instincts whereas humans have lost their instincts and are ruled by reason. What we do know about how our brain works is that we are wired to process emotion before reason. Our lives are filled with emotion; anger, sadness, happiness or envy can all make their presence felt on any given day.

It is thought to be our 'primitive brain', the limbic system, which controls our feelings and other brain functions linked to our instincts and memories. Emotions are carried out by the limbic system, which is located in the temporal lobe, while the limbic system is made up of multiple parts of the brain. The location of emotional processing is the amygdala, which receives input from other brain functions, such as memory and attention. Our primitive brain, albeit encased in a modern skull, helps us to make decisions about who to trust and makes the 'gut' reactions and decisions. Humans are essentially emotional beings. Our feelings get ahead of our thoughts and emotions always lead the race. Our initial reactions are almost always negative. This trait is a survival instinct. We are hardwired to recognise the potential for loss, injury or damage before we recognise the potential for gain.

Emotions play a role in how we behave as individuals and socially in a group. As leaders we need to be aware of these instinctive responses in ourselves and in the people around us. We are hardwired for fight or flight, the instinctive physiological response to a threatening situation, which readies us either to resist forcibly or to run away. Our first reaction to any circumstance is instinctive. We can rationalise later! Our survival instinct got us to where we are today. If we did not have this quick judgement about danger, we might not have survived as well as we have. For instance, the doctor's clinic rings about the blood test you had just recently. Your first thought will not be that they're ringing to congratulate you on lowering your cholesterol. Your first thought is likely to be: 'Oh dear, they have bad news about my health.'

When people are asked to come to a compulsory all-staff meeting, they don't immediately think: 'good news.' They are more likely to think this could mean really bad news; there will be lay-offs or the business is in trouble. The best leaders are aware of these emotions in themselves and others and they use this knowledge when communicating with their people.

THEORY OF MIND

The Theory of Mind is also highly relevant to leadership. It involves being able to attribute emotions, desires, knowledge or intent to oneself and others, and using that understanding to navigate social situations. Theory of Mind is about taking perspective and being aware that others have mental states that are possibly different from yours. It is essential in our social interactions as leaders and we use it when we judge and infer other people's behaviour. Theory of Mind is innate in apes as well as humans. This ability to take the perspective of another person was once thought to be uniquely human. Like many other attributes that have at one time or another been said to be uniquely human, it appears that other species have this ability too.

Taking another's perspective and understanding instinctive reactions is relevant to leaders as much as it is to followers. If we not only understand that others have feelings, but act upon that knowledge, our relationships will benefit. A leader who acts whilst appreciating the feelings of his or her followers will be a kinder, more compassionate leader. Similarly, followers who acknowledge that their leader and other team members have feelings and might react with emotion before thought, will also be able to make the workplace a kinder, more caring environment. This capacity to take another's perspective goes back a long way in our evolutionary history.

This capacity is evident, for example, in elephants, dolphins, Orcas, great apes and certain monkeys, as well as in some parrots and ravens, to name but a few. We mere humans have not yet worked out a test that would be uniquely appropriate for each and every species.

One test that has been used to prove Theory of Mind in great apes and some other species is the mirror test. Self-recognition is thought to be required in order to infer mental states in others. Through the sense of self we can have a sense of another's perspective. In the 1970s American psychologist Gordon Gallup was the first to use mirrors to test if primates were self-aware. During the mirror test the experimenter surreptitiously marks an animal with a dot of dye on their forehead. The animal is then presented with a mirror and their reaction is observed. A self-aware animal will touch the dot or try to remove it. This proves that the animal is aware that the reflection in the mirror is its own. All the great apes have demonstrated self-awareness via the mirror test. Elephants were not thought to have self-awareness until Joshua Plotnik gave the Asiatic Elephants at Bronx Zoo an elephant-sized mirror and a female called Happy recognised herself in it. She repeatedly rubbed the white cross marked above her eye in order to remove it.

This does not mean that the species which have not passed the mirror test are not self-aware. Assuming that the mirror test would work for all species is rather a narrow view. Dogs do not recognise themselves in a mirror, yet most dog owners will say that their dog recognises their moods and tries to console them when they are sad.

We all assume we have a mind and assume others have too. Although we don't really know what's going on in there, we attribute thoughts to others. We are able to attribute a 'state of mind' to others and we assume we can guess what others are thinking.

Chimpanzees clearly demonstrate that they have the concept of what is or may be in another's mind. The chimps in Taronga Zoo, under the previous leadership of a male called Snowy, showed Theory of Mind quite clearly. Snowy was a particularly jealous type and could not bear any of the males in the group mating with any of the females. He would severely punish any chimp caught in such an act. The lower-ranking males obviously knew Snowy's mind quite well because each time they managed what we would call a 'sneaky mating' it was in a place where Snowy could not see them. They had taken Snowy's perspective to understand what he could and could not see.

Another animal example is provided by an orangutan called Fu Manchu, a late resident of Omaha Zoo. He demonstrated an acute awareness of what others, people in his case, might or might not know. Fu Manchu was frequently found to be lounging in the tree canopy on the *outside* of his enclosure when keepers arrived in the morning. His escape plots became the stuff of legend in the zoo world and showcases a lot about intelligence and Theory of Mind in great apes.

To do what he did, Fu Manchu had to have imagination, foresight *and* Theory of Mind. He was aware of what his keepers did and did not know. High-tech surveillance finally showed how Fu managed to get out. He always waited until his caretakers went home for the night. He would then climb into an air-vent connected to his enclosure and follow the vent to a dry moat surrounding the orangutan habitat. Inside the moat there was a locked door used by keepers. Fu would then use a piece of metal wire he had in his cheek pouch to pick the lock. Persistence would have taught him how to do this, but it took planning and Theory of Mind to keep this piece of metal wire hidden from his caretakers all day – cunning abilities that show the depth of the orangutan's understanding of others' knowledge.

Good leaders use their capacity to understand that their followers have feelings that may be different from their own. Understanding 'self' and seeing others as separate 'selves' is linked to our ability to perform acts of altruism. Theory of Mind is about social competence, and social competence is related to good leadership.

EMPATHY AND COMPASSION

Empathy and compassion are aspects of Theory of Mind. Empathy and great leadership are mutually inclusive. Without taking the perspective of another we would not feel compassion or empathy. Great leaders have loyal followers but to be loyal, followers need to feel valued and validated by their leader. For followers to feel this, great leaders need to have great empathy and compassion.

In the Taronga chimp enclosure group male Samaki is a bit of a bully-boy. He often picks on little Sule, a toddler chimp. Sasha, Sule's mother, has never been very attentive. When Sule tries to escape from Samaki's rough play, she's often not around to help him out. He has others in the group to rescue him. Furahi will challenge Samaki and keep him occupied while female Lani snatches Sule and comforts him. Furahi, Lani and Sule are not family but they have all grown up in the same community. Furahi and Lani have known Sule since he was born. As he's a nice little fellow they seem fond of him and look out for him. Furahi and Lani both show the kind of empathy and that will potentially make them popular future leaders in their community.

Sule himself shows empathy too although he is only young. Koko is not a very popular chimp in the Taronga group. She was originally from another zoo and has never ranked very high in the pecking order. She gets into trouble with other chimps and is often involved in scuffles. After the melee Sule will often come over and give her a hug. They are not related. He's just an empathetic chimp.

The world we live in is obviously larger than a zoo-based chimp community. We can't show infinite empathy and compassion for every ill in the world. We do however have an innate capacity to connect with others and see their point of view. Our ability to empathise and show compassion are natural leadership qualities. The significance of empathy and compassion to leadership is that leaders are not just managing teams. They lead individuals. Leading people as individuals is key to being an effective leader.

IMPLICATIONS OF WILD LEADERSHIP FOR HUMAN LEADERSHIP TODAY

To understand what leadership is about today, we need to reflect on how it all began. Good leaders understand that our emotional reactions are as hardwired as they are in animals, and they keep this at the front of their minds.

Here's a recap of what this means for leaders:
• Aspects of hierarchy and dominance still shape human society.
• The expectations of leadership may be different between leaders and followers.
• Understanding instincts makes effective leaders.
• Theory of Mind helps us understand the impact we have on the people we lead.
• Good leaders demonstrate empathy and compassion.

In the following seven chapters different types of leadership are examined by looking at the animals that exemplify that style.

For each of these styles the following questions will be answered:

What can we learn from this leadership style?

What do the followers get from their leader?

When would we use this leadership style?

Democracy in action. Even in animals with a strict dominance structure, such as these White-faced Capuchin monkeys, any individual can propose the direction of travel. If they recruit at least three followers, the rest will follow.

Vote to hunt. African Wild Dogs have a novel way to make decisions. When resting, one or more dogs will stand up and try to rouse the rest. Those who want to move off to hunt sneeze to vote 'yes'. Once there are ten or more sneezes, the hunt begins.

African Wild Dogs' 'sneezing' to vote has obvious democratic aspects but the strongest vote is cast by one of the alpha pair. Once an alpha leader votes in favour it takes fewer votes from the pack to initiate a hunt.

Teamwork. African Wild Dogs live in complex hierarchies. They are not the strongest or fastest predator but they have excellent teamwork. When hunting as a pack, over 80 per cent of attacks end in a kill.

Meerkats in the mob fit into a linear hierarchy. Meerkat society is matriarchal and the mother calls the shots. The dominant female leads to group to food and water and is the only one to breed. All others help to raise her offspring.

Teamwork. The constant need to keep an eye and an ear out for predators makes teamwork essential. At least one meerkat will stand guard to warn of approaching dangers so others can forage and eat. This sentinel role is shared around all gang members.

Meerkat in the Kalahari, South Africa. Sharing the role of 'sentinel' helps to foster teamwork in this species.

The authoritarian leader. A Western Lowland Gorilla male exemplifies authoritarian leadership. A large and powerful leader in charge of all decisions in his troop. A gorilla silverback is often adored and feared by his followers in equal measure.

The adaptive leader.
Spotted Hyenas are gender benders and role reversers. This matriarchy can claim to be the wild founders of the #MeToo movement. Females have evolved adaptations to compete more effectively with males.

Spotted Hyena leadership is marked by a complete sex-role reversal. Females are the powerful clan leaders with the alpha supported by other high-ranking females in the sisterhood. Overthrowing the leader is very rare in Spotted Hyena society.

The laissez-faire leader. African Lion males are typically laid-back leaders who give a lot of power to the workers. Lionesses do 85 to 90 per cent of the pride's hunting while the male sleeps and rests for about 16 to 20 hours per day.

Lionesses are loyal and supportive. Although they do most of the hunting, the male lion's laissez-faire leadership style affords them social equality amongst the females. Lionesses enjoy good fellowship and even rely on each other to rear their young.

Olive Baboon males are the dominant gender but even females with low status influence where the troop goes. Troop members often follow older females because they know best where food can be found.

CHAPTER 4
THE AUTOCRATIC LEADER – GORILLA

*'Besides love and sympathy, animals exhibit
other qualities connected with the social instincts
which in us would be called moral.'*

CHARLES DARWIN

A fully-grown, angry gorilla is a fearsome sight. Early explorers such as Hanno the Navigator, a Carthaginian explorer from around 500 BC, first described what is believed to be an encounter with gorillas as: 'Savage people, the greater part of whom were women, whose bodies were hairy, and whom our interpreters called 'Gorillae'.

Throughout the ages gorillas have suffered from some significantly bad media. They are depicted in art as leaping down from trees and killing hunters and travellers. It was also believed that gorillas captured young women and ravished them in the bush. There is an interesting story about a gorilla statue created in 1859 by a French sculptor called Emmanuel Frémiet. This larger-than-life statue was entered in the exhibition of the prestigious Paris Salon. It depicted a ferocious gorilla running away with a girl tucked under his arm. So alarming was the image that the curators refused it admission to the exhibition. At the time, the work was considered too confronting given the contemporary debates about evolution. This infamous statue can now be seen at the Musée d'Arts in Nantes, France. Coincidently, the exhibition at the Paris Salon took place in the same year that Charles Darwin published his radical book *On the Origin of Species*.

This story and Darwin's work undoubtedly fed into our fascination with monster apes, resulting in movies such as *King Kong* in the last century. The 1933 Hollywood production by Merian Cooper and Ernest Schoedsack also served to give gorillas a formidable reputation. In the movie, King Kong is portrayed as crashing his way through the city, aiming to find and overpower a human female. Given these stories about gorillas and their continuing reputation in the collective imagination, it is obvious why there was much reluctance to accept that we humans were just another ape.

However, gorillas only make good movie monsters if you know nothing about them. They are also our closest living relatives, after the Bonobo and Chimpanzee, sharing 98.4 per cent of our DNA. Yet if you enter the word *gorilla* in any online thesaurus the results offer the following synonyms: *brute, thug, bully, heavy, hoodlum, hood* and *goon*. In reality gorillas are family creatures who avoid conflict.

AUTHORITARIAN LEADERSHIP – GORILLA STYLE

Gorilla males, such as my friend Kibabu, a Western Lowland Gorilla I knew in Taronga Zoo, offer an excellent example of the authoritarian leadership style. This leadership style is all about control, organisation and discipline. In Kibabu's case he's very much the benevolent dictator in his clan, the protector of his group and willing to risk his own life in order to defend members of his kin. His job is to make babies, resolve conflict, and to defend against any threats. A male gorilla leader is responsible for the wellbeing of the entire group. He, and he alone, is the one who decides everything for the group: when they move, when they feed, when they rest. This singular authority is what makes gorilla leadership autocratic and authoritarian.

Gorillas live in family groups of an alpha male, his 'wives' and their offspring. Direct supervision is the key to maintaining a successful environment in gorilla groups. The dominant male gorilla is in control at all times. This is a tough job and in the wild male gorillas only lead a family group for a few years in early adulthood when they are in peak condition.

Authoritarian or autocratic leadership was the prominent model in human society until the last hundred years or so and it is still regularly used today. A notable female leader described as having authoritarian tendencies was Margaret Thatcher. Britain's first female Prime Minister, nicknamed 'the Iron Lady', was elected in May 1979 and remained in power for eleven and a half years, making her Britain's longest serving Prime Minister of the 20th century.

Similarly, Russian President Vladimir Putin is often mentioned as an example of a contemporary 'strong man' leader. Putin's authoritarian style may stem from his reported background as a former KGB agent. In some male-dominated societies, such as Hungary, Turkey, Armenia and Saudi Arabia to name a few, the authoritarian leadership style is still very prevalent.

UNDERSTANDING LANGUAGE — DUTCH TO ENGLISH

The gorilla group in Taronga Zoo came from a famous zoo in the Netherlands – Apenheul Primate Park. To help the group settle in, zookeepers and vets from Taronga Zoo travelled to the Netherlands to get to know the gorillas. Additionally, keepers from Apenheul Primate Park travelled with the group and stayed in Sydney for several months to make the transition to the family's new home as smooth as possible. The Dutch keepers taught the 'Dutch' gorillas the new language they now had to understand. They repeated each request given in Dutch, such as 'go outside please' or 'come inside please', in English. This way the group would understand the requests of their new Australian carers. Under the leadership of Kibabu, the gorillas learned their new language in a matter of days. When asked by carers to come inside, for example, Kibabu showed the way each time; he would be the first to react and if he agreed with the request, the females and youngsters would follow his lead.

THE LEADER AS PROTECTOR

Early one morning in the spring of 2006, Kibabu showed exemplary leadership during a dramatic event. Keepers arriving for their morning shift saw smoke billowing out of the gorilla night house. The fire brigade was called and meanwhile staff climbed onto the roof to break the plastic skylights and let the smoke out. When the fire brigade arrived the secured building was unlocked for them to enter. Two fire officers disappeared into the smoke clad in their protective gear and toting their breathing apparatus.

Kibabu and his family must have been terrified. Nothing in their experience could have prepared them for this sight. When Kibabu saw the firemen appearing through the smoke he must have thought a great danger was about to befall his family. The firemen in their helmets and fluoro uniforms probably looked like aliens. He charged with all his power, smacking the mesh and screaming at the top of his lungs. The fire officers were in such a hurry to get out of the building at that point that the two guys fell over each other with the oxygen tanks on their backs, scrambling to get back on their feet. Only once safely outside did they regain their composure. The fire was actually quite minimal, the plumes of smoke resulting from a minor electrical fault in the kitchen, and was soon extinguished.

Despite his own fear, when the smoke began to accumulate, Kibabu guided his entire clan of eleven out of a series of interconnected bedrooms to the 'playroom'. The playroom roof is open to the sky and the only place in whole building allowing access to fresh air. That pocket of air kept them alive until the fire was extinguished and the smoke cleared. Kibabu knew the safest place to take his family to protect them. As soon as possible, we let all the animals exit the building to their outdoor habitat to get some clean air. But once Kibabu led his troop outside he wasn't letting them back into the building. It took a couple of weeks before he allowed the group to go back inside, lured only by yummy foods. Kibabu's conduct was an extraordinary example of an authoritarian leader who is also brave and caring.

HOW GORILLA SOCIETY WORKS

Gorillas are the largest and most powerful of the great apes and live in relatively stable social groups. Typically a family consists of a strong adult male, a harem of three or four females and their combined offspring, often three to six youngsters. Male gorillas develop silver-coloured hair on their back and thighs as they mature. After that they are called 'silverbacks'. A silverback is usually at least twelve years old. They have large canine teeth which also develop with maturity.

Gorillas display significant sexual dimorphism. The size difference between the silverback and the females is enormous. The male may weigh 180–200kg (400–440lb) whereas females are at least 50 per cent smaller and usually weigh 70–90kg (150–200lb). In the wild, silverbacks are challenged by other males on a regular basis. A typical silverback has the strength of several grown men and he's prepared to use that physical power to defend his family and his position. Competition is the likely reason males are so much bigger than females, with natural selection favouring sexual dimorphism between the sexes. This size difference characteristic is shared with many other polygamous mammals, such as seals and lions, where one male dominates several females. A silverback also uses his size to keep control of his harem.

As an aside perhaps, thinking about the size difference between males and females in societies where males dominate has some potentially interesting parallels in our world. A coincidence perhaps, but I have always been intrigued with the fashion that developed once feminism became more entrenched in our world and more women worked and had careers. In the 1980s, women in the western world had big hair, big shoulder pads, bright coloured clothes and platform shoes. Were we trying to match the size of dominant, authoritarian males in the workplace?

Anyway... The dominant male gorilla is a true authoritarian and makes all the decisions. He closely watches the members of his group and will correct their conduct if he thinks it is wrong. Usually, a stare or head jerk from him will be enough to keep the peace. It's the silverback who maintains social harmony. Adult females are only dominant over young animals. A female's rank may depend on how long she has been in the group and her reproductive status. Females tend to avoid each other and if they can't they often squabble either verbally or physically. If two females are fighting, the silverback will immediately jump in to separate them. Sometimes he punishes the culprit but mostly he reprimands both, as if he does not much care who started it as long as the bickering stops. An experienced male gorilla will be gentle but firm in managing conflict resolution.

After a fight, the females are unlikely to reconcile with each other as Chimpanzees or Bonobos would, but they will try very hard to appease the silverback. Females all want to be in the good books with the authoritarian male who is the all-knowing and all-powerful figure in their lives. As a consequence, the females spend much more time in proximity to the male than they do with each other. A female with young in particular will aim to be close to the silverback. He protects her and her baby from the unwanted approaches of other males. Related females in a troop, such as mother and daughter, tend to be friendlier towards each other and associate more closely. Otherwise, unrelated females have few friendly encounters.

The bond that a silverback has with his females is the core of gorilla social life. Bonds between the male and his females are maintained by grooming and sitting close together. The silverback is the focus of everybody's attention, making the decisions, mediating conflicts, determining the movements of the group and taking responsibility for the safety and well-being of the troop. However, Kibabu despite being ruler and enforcer, also has his softer side. He can often be seen playing games with the youngsters in the group. Despite his enormous strength he is ever so gentle with the infants in the family. Kibabu demonstrates that the authoritarian leader can show a soft and gentle side without losing respect.

BACHELOR GORILLAS

Young gorilla males aged between eight and twelve years are called blackbacks and lack silver back hair. These youngsters are subordinate to the silverback and help out with protection of the clan in times of trouble. There are plenty of bachelors in gorilla society as the gorilla social structure has one silverback monopolising a harem. However, the birth-ratio is about 50:50 in terms of male to female births. As few males possess a harem of females and most males none at all, competition for access to female gorillas is fierce. This results in many males with no harem to lead. Some such juniors stay in proximity to family groups, biding their time until they believe they have what it takes to challenge the leading silverback. Other males, often young or very old, hang out in bachelor groups. They have friendly interactions and socialise with the other bachelors through play, grooming and staying together. Occasionally they engage in homosexual interactions.

POPULAR JAPANESE ROLE MODELS

The authoritarian leadership style is still popular in parts of the world. Male gorilla Shabani grew up in Taronga Zoo, Australia, and transferred to Japan to breed with unrelated female gorillas in Nagoya Higashiyama Zoo. Shabani has become a national heart-throb in Japan after thousands of young girls went bananas on Twitter about his 'decisiveness and good looks'. Shabani clearly demonstrates his authoritarian leadership in the way he manages his troop. He does so gently though. In fact, Shabani is so admired, so handsome, that officials have credited him with a massive spike in female visitor numbers to the Nagoya Higashiyama Zoo and Botanical Gardens. A book was published about him that sold out in weeks and is now in its third print-run. His charismatic authoritarian leadership style is still admired and a popular role-model in some human societies.

SEX IN GORILLA SOCIETY

Making all the decisions and being the alpha is a tough job. In the wild male gorillas often only lead a family group for a limited time. Alphas are in peak condition in early adulthood when they lead a family. Zoos aim to replicate what happens in the wild and that means making sure that a capable virile male leads the group. It is also necessary to maintain genetic diversity in the breeding program and individuals must not have too many offspring with the same genetic make-up. When my old friend Kibabu reached his thirties he had sired fourteen offspring and the time came to retire him from his duties. Introducing a new male to the existing females is a tricky job. If the females don't like him it can take a long time to establish harmony in the group again.

A new silverback may also kill any youngsters in the group as he is keen to get the females cycling again so as to produce his own offspring. Zoos therefore make sure there are no young under the age of about four or five in the group so that the transfer of leadership can happen without aggression or injuries to youngsters. The females in the Kibabu group were therefore placed on a contraceptive for a couple of years. This was done to make sure no new babies were born for a while in preparation for the arrival of a new silverback.

Sexually receptive female gorillas will purse their lips and slowly approach the male while making eye contact. This serves to urge the male to mount her. If the male does not respond, then she will try to attract his attention by reaching towards him or slapping the ground. Males incite mating by approaching a female and displaying at her, showing off essentially with chest-beating, slapping the ground or touching her. Gorillas have been observed engaging in face-to-face sex, a sexual position once considered unique to humans and Bonobos.

When Kibabu's harem of gorilla girls had been on contraception for some months they appeared to get restless, perhaps as a result of the lack of sexual action. Mouila, Frala and Kriba, the gorilla girls, seemed to blame this lack of action and baby-making on poor Kibabu. Perhaps they thought he was losing interest in mating or was infertile. Unusually, the females would join forces to give Kibabu a hard time every now and then. They took their frustration out on him and would bite his feet when he was having a quiet nap, even chasing him around occasionally. In the wild, such behaviour would have led to another male in the area taking over the alpha role. We were able to retire Kibabu more gracefully to a small zoo on the coast with his favourite female.

The example of Kibabu shows that even under authoritarian leadership, followers can band together to gang up on the leader if he is not considered up to the job. Making babies is one such job for a gorilla male.

HOW CLOSELY RELATED ARE WE TO GORILLAS?

The DNA difference between humans and gorillas is 1.6 per cent – a little more than the difference between us and Chimpanzees and Bonobos. As in human biology, births can take place any time of the year. The female gorilla's menstrual cycle is on average 32 days and lasts around two to three days. Females are pregnant for an average of 256 days, compared to the human gestation of 280 days.

Gorillas in human care can be given most medications that are developed for humans. Our anatomy is very similar and zoos will often use human specialists such as gynaecologists, paediatricians or cardiologists to diagnose and treat ailments in the great apes in their care. Gorillas are also susceptible to most diseases that are contagious in humans. They are naive to some of these diseases, such as the common cold, so in zoos we have to be very careful not to spread our colds and flus to them as it can make them very sick. Any person with a cold or a cough is usually banned from direct contact with the gorillas.

EMOTIONS IN GORILLAS

When you work closely with gorillas or other great apes you recognise many emotions that we too would feel under the same circumstances. A poignant example of grieving was seen in gorilla mother, Gana, in Münster Zoo, Germany. Gana was cradling her three-month old baby son, Claudio, when he died suddenly from a possible heart defect. Marcus Dunk, writing for the *Daily Mail*, described the scene as follows:

'Holding the lifeless body of her dead child like a rag doll, this female gorilla stares at the corpse in shock and bewilderment, unable to accept that her baby is dead. For hours the distraught mother gently shook and stroked the child, vainly seeking to restore movement to his lolling head and limp arms. Visitors to the zoo openly wept as they witnessed her actions. Hours passed, during which Gana continually prodded and caressed the dead child, to no effect.

It is a picture of pure grief. Inconsolable, hers is the raw pain of any mother who has lost a child. While nature may indeed be red in tooth and claw, this moving image of Gana and her dead son Claudio seems to show that members of the animal kingdom can feel the pain of loss just as deeply as we humans.

Gorillas have a strong attachment to their offspring and mourn the death of loved ones. Often gorilla mothers will carry their dead baby for hours or even days, until it begins to decompose. Gorilla mothers who lose a baby will show grief in many ways. Their posture will appear lethargic, they lose interest in food and mope about. When we see these behaviours it is impossible *not* to think that these animals are just like us. We experience many of the same emotions as other intelligent, social species.

WHAT CAN WE LEARN FROM GORILLA AUTHORITARIAN LEADERSHIP?

Authoritarian leadership style is characterised by one individual's control over all decisions with little input from anybody else. Just like a silverback! Authoritarian leaders make decisions based on their ideas and judgments alone and rarely seek advice from followers. Like all leadership styles, the authoritarian style model has pros and cons. These leaders can be seen as overly bossy or dictatorial. When and where this authoritarian style is most helpful depends on the situation, the task at hand and personalities of the team members.

In gorilla groups, followers are often in constant competition with each other for the attention of the silverback. The females squabble over food and access to their leader. There is a loose hierarchy of some sort which can be seen especially when the group moves in a single file, with more dominant females taking the front positions. But this somewhat vague pecking order does not help to resolve the conflicts between them as it might in other social apes where a truer hierarchy is evident.

There are circumstances when the authoritarian leadership style can be the right one to use. I have used it for instance when a potentially harmful animal is loose in the zoo and there really is no time for a nice discussion of 'What we do now?' Training in emergency response takes over and commands are given with the expectation they be followed. This leadership style can be effective when there is no time to talk and there needs to be a fast response to an urgent situation. The authoritarian leadership style might be domineering but it can be useful in critical situations, such as during an emergency. For group members it can, at such times, be beneficial to concentrate on performing the task without having to make complex decisions. It also allows a team working under this leadership style to become highly skilled at performing certain duties, such as during military conflict.

This leadership style can also be useful in manufacturing or similar industries where all involved have clearly assigned tasks, deadlines to meet and safety rules to follow. It may do well in these situations because it can prevent injuries and get projects finished on time. The downside of this style is that it can come across as dictatorial, resulting in resentment in followers. Highly-skilled people may feel that their contributions are not valued under this leadership. Researchers have also found that authoritarian leaders may lack creative solutions to problems, overlooking the expertise the group may bring to the situation. People tend to be happier in their work if they feel they are making a contribution to the team or the success of the business. While authoritarian leaders typically avoid seeking input, followers may feel dissatisfied and the group may have low morale.

In zoos, if a silverback unexpectedly dies and leaves the group without a leader, the friction between the remaining animals in the group will increase dramatically. Without an authoritarian leader to keep the peace, group harmony is seriously at risk. The troop has not learned to self-regulate and come up with rules to keep the peace. The same can happen in workplaces where a forceful boss makes all the decisions. If the boss is not around there may be decision paralysis or so much competition that efficiency is impacted.

What we can learn from the gorilla example of this leadership style, however, is the leader's complete devotion to his clan. His commitment to their wellbeing is paramount. He brings harmony to the group and is gentle but firm when he has to be.

Although a silverback has many privileges it should also be remembered that they live hard and often shorter lives than males who do not lead a troop. Humans have choices in leadership styles.

We can rationalise how we want to lead. We have several models in our primate relatives, gorillas being only *one* example. Although it may be tempting sometimes to simply issue the order, 'Just do it,' like Kibabu would, we also have other choices we can employ to suit the situation and the team.

GORILLAS ON THE RED LIST

The International Union for Conservation of Nature (IUCN) Red List of Threatened Species lists two species of gorillas, further divided into four subspecies.

Western Gorilla (*Gorilla gorilla*)
  Western Lowland Gorilla (*G. g. gorilla*)
  Cross River Gorilla (*G. g. diehli*)
Eastern Gorilla (*Gorilla beringei*)
  Mountain Gorilla (*G. b. beringei*)
  Eastern Lowland Gorilla or Grauer's Gorilla (*G. b. graueri*)

All four subspecies are either classified as 'Endangered' or 'Critically Endangered' – threatened by hunting for bushmeat, habitat loss, wildlife trade and infectious diseases.

Many gorilla populations have significantly declined or disappeared in recent times. The lowland subspecies are more numerous than the highland and mountain subspecies. Mountain Gorillas are the only gorillas to have shown a moderate increase in numbers, but the overall population size is still very low.

The Western Lowland Gorilla is the most widespread, possibly numbering 100,000.

The Cross River Gorilla is currently the world's rarest great ape, with a population of only around 250–300 restricted to a small area of highland forest on the border of Cameroon and Nigeria.

The population of the Eastern Lowland Gorilla has crashed in recent decades and is now under 4,000.

The total population of Mountain Gorillas is around 880 individuals, split into two separate groups.

WHAT DO GORILLA FOLLOWERS EXPECT FROM THEIR AUTHORITARIAN LEADER?

First and foremost gorilla females want a leader who protects them and their offspring from any danger. Danger may come from a hungry Leopard or from a lone male gorilla who may wish to take over the troop. The silverback will fight to the death to protect his family. Female gorillas therefore vie to be near their silverback at all times. The closer they are the more protection they have, so access and proximity to him is important.

Secondly, they expect the silverback to lead them to good places to feed, rest and sleep.

Thirdly, they expect the leader to swiftly resolve disharmony in the troop as the females have a weak hierarchy order amongst themselves. They bond more with their dominant male than with each other and have frequent disagreements. It is important to them to have a leader who resolves that conflict and restores peace in the group. They want a male who does this job fairly and without aggression.

WHEN WOULD WE USE THE AUTHORITARIAN LEADERSHIP STYLE?

While the authoritarian leadership model has some pitfalls, leaders can use elements of this style to their benefit, for example when time is critical and where the leader is the most expert member of the team. The expert leader is able to make fast decisions rather than wasting time consulting with less knowledgeable team members. This style is best used in specific situations as part of a larger suite of leadership tools. Balancing this approach with other styles such as democratic leadership can often lead to better group satisfaction and outcomes.

The example of the male gorilla may imply a masculine approach to some readers. What does this example of the authoritarian style mean for female leaders? The answer is: exactly the same as for male leaders. Leadership styles are not gender specific. It is the *intention* behind the leadership style that is important. We can use the positive attributes of the style in the right circumstances and with the right people whilst ignoring the potentially negative traits.

In humans, the authoritarian leadership style may not result in harmony in the group without the constant supervision of the leader and correction of any aberrant behaviour amongst followers. In business and politics, an authoritarian leader is defined as someone who sets individual goals for the group and engages primarily in one-way and downward communication. An authoritarian leader controls all discussions within the group and dominates all interactions. Not that different from the way that silverbacks go about business.

It is not all that long ago that most leaders in our western culture were authoritarian. It is only in relatively recent times that equality has become more desirable. People in feudal times would not have dreamt of equality, whereas now we expect the workplace, in particular, to be more equal and democratic.

Several studies have confirmed a relationship between bullying on the one hand, and an autocratic leadership or authoritarian way of settling conflicts on the other. An authoritarian style of leadership may create a climate of fear, where there is little or no room for dialogue and where complaining may be considered futile. This definition rings true for gorillas: while a male gorilla may be adored by his family group, he is usually feared in equal measure.

The authoritarian male may be challenged by other males wanting his position. In gorillas we would see posturing between the males, especially the silverback, who must scare off the challenging male. We see this in the posturing of humans too. I have been in many meetings where some people, men in particular, use posture to increase their physical size. They may lean back in the chair, 'manspread' with legs wide open, and even place their hands behind their head to increase the shape of their overall presence in the room. Perhaps this also serves to spread the male hormone odours from the armpit and the groin to the room.

Many of us have also seen people display like an angry gorilla when they believe their power is being threatened or questioned. The male gorilla will beat his chest, roar and pull up vegetation to throw around. The display ends with the gorilla thumping the ground with the palms of his hands. This is not so dissimilar to a human talking more loudly, even yelling, banging the table or throwing the meeting papers violently on the table or slamming the door.

If everybody panders to the authoritarian leader there is little to no incentive for group cohesion in his or her absence. If all group members must compete for the attention and approval of the leader to gain privileges, team-building becomes all but impossible. There are times and circumstances that call for this leadership style, such as in urgent situations demanding decisiveness for protection and safety. But the domineering side of this style should probably only be used sparingly under extreme conditions that warrant immediate and obedient action.

GORILLA MEMORY

Gorillas are not naturally as inquisitive as Chimpanzees but they have good memories. One of our young males, Haoko, was transferred to a zoo in Tokyo, Japan, to become a breeding male there. A couple of months after his big move I went over to see how well he was settling in. Although I had not been working directly with the gorillas for some time while Haoko was in Taronga Zoo, I visited the gorilla house regularly. I did not think that Haoko would recognise me, but as soon as he saw me and heard my voice he came running over to get a closer look. He then gave some lovely low rumbling sounds – a friendly sign of recognition. I felt he knew I had come from his old home and he showed his appreciation. Although I was touched by his recognition, I will never know what he recognised. Did he see a western face among the Japanese ones? Did he recognise my face or my voice? I like to think he thought he saw an old friend...

CHAPTER 5

THE ADAPTABLE LEADER – SPOTTED HYENA

'I never thought that finding myself confined in a small space with a Spotted Hyena would be good news, but there you go.'

YANN MARTEL, *LIFE OF PI*.

Spotted Hyenas are the wild founders of the *#MeToo* movement. Their societies could even be said to be at the extreme end of the *#MeToo* spectrum. Females control males. They have no vaginal opening but do have a fully erectile clitoris that looks like a penis! An evolutionary enigma in many aspects, hyenas are an example of what adaptive leadership can look like. Hyenas are neither canine nor feline. They are carnivores but often behave like primates. They have the most beautiful eyes, doggy-like wet noses and they can take your leg off in one bite! People have strange beliefs about hyenas. It's been said that they have magical powers and that witches rode on their backs. We seem to admire hunters like the noble Lion and the fast Cheetah but hyenas, known generally as scavengers, get a bad rap in the media.

Even the author Ernest Hemingway, in his book *Green Hills of Africa*, commented on the hyena as: 'Devourer of the dead, trailer of calving cows, ham-stringer, potential biter-off of your face at night while you sleep, sad yowler, camp-follower, stinking, foul, with jaws that crack the bones the lion leaves, belly dragging, loping away on the brown plain.' I think we can safely assume that Hemingway was not fond of hyenas. Even in the 1994 animated classic Walt Disney movie *The Lion King*, hyenas are portrayed as conniving and cowardly thieves who are also 'slobbery, mangy and stupid.' The three Spotted Hyenas in the film, Shenzi, Banzai and Ed, are henchmen and while every good movie needs its villains, the reputation of the Spotted Hyena suffered again as a consequence of their portrayal in this one. The repute of scavengers, like hyenas and vultures, is never very positive but these species are in fact nature's cleaners and garbage collectors and we need them. Besides, almost all carnivores will scavenge, even the noble Lion, if they come across a dead animal that a rival has taken down.

Although they do scavenge at times, hyenas, contrary to popular belief, are excellent hunters and catch 60 to 90 per cent of their food. Hyenas are also utterly fascinating and seriously misunderstood mammals. James Bruce, a Scottish travel writer who spent more than a dozen years in North Africa and Ethiopia during the 1800s, reputedly said: 'There are few animals whose history has passed under the consideration of naturalists that have given occasion to so much confusion and equivocation as the hyena has done.'

Although they look mostly like dogs, the four species of hyena – the Spotted, Striped and Brown Hyenas and the Aardwolf – are more closely related to cats and even more closely to mongooses and civets. The Spotted Hyena, also known as the laughing hyena, is the best known, the most numerous and the most unusual. Their maniacal 'laugh' is a high-pitched cackle that is used when they are excited or scared. Although they are often viewed with revulsion, hyenas live a life devoted to family and clan.

ADAPTIVE LEADERSHIP – SPOTTED HYENA STYLE

The hyena leadership style can be described as *adaptive*. Spotted Hyenas are gender benders and role reversers. Hyenas have evolved some very unusual adaptations to better suit their environment. The adaptive leadership style obviously has advantages as the species is highly successful. Evolutionary biologists believe that Spotted Hyena adaptations over time are a response to the poor survival of cubs. Female dominance in particular is likely to be an evolutionary adaptation to compete with males for food, making sure they can produce enough milk to feed their cubs. The cubs take a long time to grow sufficiently strong jaws to feed off carcasses directly, and the mother is responsible for feeding them during this time. With female dominance, the access to food for cubs is more secure. Female coalitions keep control of the clan members and are quick to punish misbehaviour, particularly in males.

An alpha female is the top-ranking animal in the clan, supported by other high rankers in the sisterhood. The hierarchy is most obvious at feeding time. Once the kill is made other clan members will join to get their share of the prey. The alpha always has first dibs on the good bits and can eat her fill. This is why cubs of higher-ranked animals have better survival chances than those of lower-ranked mothers (note the similarities with human families with higher socio-economic status!). In hyenas, as in some primates, an individual's position in the hierarchy strongly determines its priority of access to food. The dominant leaders practice nepotism and the offspring of a high-ranking female will, like royalty, outrank adult females that are subordinate to their mother.

In any travelling subgroup, the highest-ranked female hyena leads the group. High-ranking hyenas attract more followers. This makes sense because philopatric adult female hyenas (those who stay in the natal clan) are likely to have greater social and ecological knowledge than other young females or adult males who have recently immigrated from neighbouring social groups. In hyena travelling parties, there may be a rule that says, 'follow the adult female that outranks me' because low-ranking females have less social capital.

Indeed, female elders, presumably with the most local knowledge, often enlist more followers than young, naive individuals in many mammal species. High-ranking hyena females benefit from the help of followers, such as with assistance during the hunt and defending their kills from Lions or neighbouring clans. Although high-ranking leaders benefit more from being followed than low-ranking followers gain from following, this ranked society may increase the efficiency of group decisions. Hyenas rely upon fairly passive, rather than overt, leadership during hunts or reunions. All adult females in the clan are habitual leaders during hunts for example. Interestingly, lactating females are significantly more likely to assume leadership roles during a hunt than are non-lactating females. A lactating female has to find food to produce milk to feed her offspring. She has more 'skin in the game', and therefore will always have more street cred.

Alternatively, lactating female hyenas may gather more followers because they spend a lot of time close to the communal den – the social hub where clan members gather to socialise. Lactating females are likely to visit the communal dens more often than other clan members because they must feed their young cubs in a place that is safe. Generally, research has shown that young adults and immigrant males were most likely to be followers during hunts or reunions with other clan hyenas.

The clan is a fission-fusion society in which clan members separate and come together again on a regular basis. Despite hyena social complexity, the subgroups in this fission-fusion society may be 'self-organised' in that the clans appear to lack an overall leader who makes travel decisions. Instead, as in self-organised flocks of birds, coordinated travel may be based on local decisions. The highest-ranking adult female in each subgroup of hyenas is most often the leader at a given time.

Nepotism is rife in the animal world and thus it is not surprising that it is ubiquitous and difficult to control in our own societies. Power in hyenas is a family affair as the alpha is most likely to have inherited her mother's territories and social position. It is interesting to note that this 'royal' passing down of power from mother to daughter applies more to Spotted Hyenas than to supposedly regal animals such as the Lion. Because the alpha leader has first access to food, she can feed her offspring better than any other clan member. More of her offspring will survive and those offspring will also rank high in the clan and support the alpha in maintaining her top job – a vicious circle of dominance being reinforced by the perks of the top job. Tendencies for dominance start early in life, stronger cubs even killing weaker ones in power struggles. Anna Bennett has worked with Spotted Hyenas in Monarto Zoo, Australia. She has filmed Spotted Hyena births and observed sibling fighting start immediately after a twin birth.

Hyenas are also highly adaptive when it comes to food. They are known as opportunistic feeders and almost anything is on the menu – fur, feathers, wings or scales. They even eat the dung of African Wild Dogs and wildebeests. Prey species can be three times as big as the hyena – they will take on zebras, young giraffes and wildebeest. A female hyena can run down, tackle and kill a bull wildebeest many times her own weight, all on her own. They also kill and eat birds, lizards, snakes and insects. Hyenas have enormously strong jaws and can crush the bones and other tough parts of a kill – nothing goes to waste.

Hans Kruuk, a noted Spotted Hyena researcher, studied the species in Tanzania in the 1960s, resulting in the first publication of a comprehensive study in 1972. In his book, *The Spotted Hyena*, he relates the following story:

'Suddenly one hyena managed to grab a young zebra while the stallion was chasing another member of the pack. This young zebra, which was between nine and twelve months old, fell back a little, and within seconds twelve hyenas converged on it; in

30 seconds they had pulled it down while the rest of the family ran slowly on. More hyenas arrived, and the little zebra was completed covered by them. At 19.17 hours, ten minutes after the victim had been caught, the last hyena carried off the head and nothing remained on the spot but a dark patch on the grass and some stomach contents. Twenty-five hyenas were involved and the dismembering took exactly seven minutes.'

The speed with which hyenas devour a carcass is an adaptation that prevents the prey item being claimed by Lions or other hunters on the plains. The way the hyena communities are led, how they hunt and what they hunt, can all be attributed to being a highly adaptive species.

HOW SPOTTED HYENA SOCIETY WORKS

Spotted Hyena society is marked by a dominance hierarchy and complete sex-role reversal. This society is both female philopatric and matriarchal. Females are larger than males by up to 10 per cent. This sexual dimorphism is typically expressed by females looking more robust than males. High-ranking hyenas maintain their position through aggression towards lower-ranking clan members. Females dominate males and even the lowest-ranking females are dominant over the highest-ranking male. All hyena cubs outrank any adult male. As females stay in their birth clan, the large clans have several matrilines. Rank reversal and overthrowing the leader is very rare in Spotted Hyena clans as linear dominance hierarchies can be fairly stable.

Hyenas are highly social and live in multi-generational clans with sometimes 90 or more individuals who defend a common territory. Clans are divided up into smaller hunting packs and individuals, but all members are evidently recognisable to each other. Group sizes vary considerably subject to what prey is around. Clans are smaller in territories where the prey is migratory, whilst in territories where prey is resident all year round clans are bigger. The success of the hyena may be due in part to its adaptability as it can make a living by both hunting and scavenging. Hyenas can hunt alone, in small groups of two to five, or in much larger clans.

Multiple males and females can breed and young are deposited in a communal den when they are about one month old. The communal den is the centre of social activity for the clan. Older hyenas visit the dens regularly, which gives the cubs opportunities to learn about the strict hierarchy in which they live. Spotted Hyenas recognise their kin and others of the clan as individuals. They seem to know how each individual ranks against others in the clan and they use this knowledge adaptively to make social decisions about who is who and how they and others fit into the hierarchy.

The clan gets involved in territory patrols, scent marking the borders with a paste from an anal gland to make sure neighbouring clans know not to overstep the marked area. The whole clan may get involved with this activity and it probably provides good social bonding. One would also need quite a few clan members to have enough anal gland secretions to mark an entire border!

Bonding is an element of all social groups and an important aspect in its cohesion. Studies by Jennifer Smith and colleagues looked at how Spotted Hyenas are able to sort out conflict over rank after separations. Each time a subgroup separates from the clan and goes off on a hunt they have a temporary leader. Those leaders are the ones initiating greetings during subsequent reunions. Hyena reunions are full of excitement. Conflict is common as reunions often happen around a fresh kill. Leaders with a high rank will often initiate fights as well as greetings.

Greetings usually reduce conflict just as they do in humans and other primates. Greetings involve nuzzling, muzzle licking and body rubs. More formally, a lower-ranking animal will lift its leg to allow the dominant one to sniff or lick its under-carriage, an obviously risky proposition but a demonstration of trust. Other subordinate gestures include grovelling and head bobbing.

Greeting is a theme that returns time and time again in animal societies. Greetings are used to bond, to reaffirm relationships, to confirm who the leader is and to perform other social functions. These animal rituals relay a really important message for us too. Greeting our clan or colleagues is an important aspect of our sociality too and demonstrated by the ingrained greeting behaviour in social animals. Even when we are busy, it should be of significant importance to stop what we are doing, make eye contact and say hello. At least we don't have to lift a leg!

Conflict happens in all social groups and resolving it quickly is vital so that relationships are not damaged permanently. Conflict undermines the cohesion of the entire group, beyond those directly involved in the disagreement. Reconciling is a valuable social mechanism that helps regulate relationships and reduces social tension. Hyenas have a way of making up after an altercation, which benefits the community as a whole. After a squabble the behaviours seen are initiating play, sniffing, greeting and other non-aggressive approaches. Similarly, we shouldn't allow arguments to fester in our workplaces. We should follow the example of hyenas and make up as soon as possible to keep the relationship from being damaged beyond repair. This counts for leaders as much as it does for followers.

HYENA PHYSICAL ATTRIBUTES AND HOW THEY MIGHT HAVE DEVELOPED

The evolutionary war between the sexes has resulted in some drastic adaptations in hyenas. Perhaps the strangest thing about female Spotted Hyenas is the masculinised anatomy of their genitalia. On the inside there is the normal mammalian reproductive equipment but their external genitalia are bizarre. There is no external vaginal opening – a truly unique feature in a mammal. Instead, the clitoris is elongated to the point that it forms a fully erectile pseudo-penis. This multi-tasking organ is used to urinate, copulate and give birth through. That all sounds perfectly alright until you get to the 'birthing' part. Between one and three cubs, exit through the clitoris birth canal which is only about 2.5cm (1in) in diameter.

For centuries people speculated that Spotted Hyena were hermaphrodite, having both male and female sex organs, or alternatively that they were male for part of their lives and then female. They were observed with both swollen mammary glands for milk production and what look like a large phallic erection. This has been confusing people for some time. 'Nobody really understands yet quite what it is there for,' says Kay Holekamp, a biologist who has been studying Spotted Hyenas for more than twenty years in Masai Mara National Reserve in Kenya. One theory is that female hyenas, through the species' evolution, have been naturally selected for a larger size and aggression. Nearing the end of gestation, high-ranking females flush their embryos with androgen, a male sex hormone linked to aggression. The high levels of male hormone during embryonic development could make their genitals develop the unusual features. This anatomical structure additionally gives them full control over sexual activities and partners. Non-consensual sex is impossible with this anatomy – the female's full cooperation is needed for proper coitus to happen. Apart from a clitoris that looks like a penis, the female's labia are fused to form two fatty pads that look like a scrotum. The appearance is so similar that gender can only really be ascertained by palpation of the scrotum – if one is present – an obviously tricky proposal!

The Spotted Hyena is an adaptable species like no other.

WHAT CAN WE LEARN FROM SPOTTED HYENA ADAPTIVE LEADERSHIP?

Over millions of years of evolution, hyenas have developed an unparalleled ability to adapt their anatomy, physiology and culture to better suit their circumstances and environment. Cub survival was an issue so they did something about it in a drastic way. The adaptive leadership style obviously has some advantages as the species is highly successful in its environment. It is the most common large carnivore in Africa and has been around for 24 million years. Hyena social organisation bears no resemblance to that of any other carnivore, being more like that of baboons or macaques in terms of group size, hierarchical structure and social interaction. This species, more than others, has come up with novel, adaptive ways to overcome societal problems, although its dominance structure is inflexible.

Kay Holekamp of Michigan State University says: 'By studying an animal that seems to contradict the usual rules, you can shed light on what the rules really are. Plus, I just think they're really cool.' Evolution in this species has come up with many alternative adaptations to the pressures of living in an environment that already has a number of proficient predators.

In our society, the adaptive leadership style may suit in circumstances where a completely new approach is needed and where people don't have a rigid world view. It can be useful when the old ways just don't bring desirable results and the team is not thriving. Change can be slow, but a steady approach to an alternative path can bring success.

FISSION-FUSION SOCIETIES

In ethology – the study of animal behaviour – we often talk about fission-fusion societies. In many species this is a common strategy that allows flexible social organisation. The flexibility lets group members hang out with subgroups or preferred individuals. Groups get together (fusion) and separate again (fission) as they move around to forage or hunt. The group size and composition changes frequently. Chimpanzees, for example, often forage alone or in small groups and may come together again at night to sleep. As a result, group composition in a lot of species is very dynamic. Social groups can divide into small parties of perhaps a few individuals and social parties can also fuse with other groups to form aggregations of hundreds of animals.

While this flexible social organisation is not the norm amongst all primates, it is characteristic of human societies and those of Chimpanzees and Bonobos. It is also seen in a wide range of other species, such as African Elephants, African Lions, Plains Zebra, giraffes, Bottlenose Dolphins, Spotted Hyenas, some birds such as the Great Tit, and even fish like guppies.

WHAT DO SPOTTED HYENA FOLLOWERS EXPECT FROM THEIR ADAPTIVE LEADER?

The followers under this kind of leader both benefit and are disadvantaged to some degree. If you are a female, your cubs are more likely to survive. Females receive protection from the coalitions they form. Males that harass females in heat are often attacked and chased away by high-ranking female clan members. Males that find most reproductive success are those that have fostered a relationship with the female over a longer period of time

– a complex behaviour bearing similarities to human interactions.

If you are a hyena male there are obviously less-positive aspects to this society. Male hyenas are kept on a short leash. Adult males eat last at a kill and they risk violent punishment from the female coalitions for any perceived misdemeanour. If a male hunts dinner on his own he must eat quickly before a female clan member finds him and pushes him aside. Males disperse from their natal clan at puberty. Until they leave the clan they enjoy the privileges of their mother's rank. When they leave, they have to beg for acceptance in another clan and even if successful they are kept on 'probation' for a period of time. Biologists call this 'endurance rivalry'. If the male sticks with it for long enough he may eventually get a female to mate with. His probation can last a couple of years, after which the lowest ranking female may allow a mating. Being a male Spotted Hyena is very tough!

Hyena females choose their male partners according to several criteria. They prefer immigrant males over those born within the clan – a measure to prevent inbreeding. Male rank does not necessarily influence their reproductive success, but females do show a preference for males that are of similar age, are submissive and less aggressive. The selection of less aggressive males may further perpetuate the difference between the sexes.

Infanticide by males is unfortunately common in the animal world. Female hyenas copulate with several males when in heat, possibly to let them all think they are the father and minimise the potential for infanticide. They can choose the sire of their offspring and sexual non-consent is impossible through the pseudo-penis. Cubs in one litter may have several fathers.

Their success as a species is underpinned by biological mechanisms, a unique anatomy and flexibility. The females have evolved to ensure cub survival by being bigger than the males, more aggressive and therefore able to eat first. Their flexibility in hunting techniques means that they can scavenge or hunt alone, in a small group, or in a large pack, and consume every part of the kill, even bones. Furthermore, by forming female-led coalitions, leaders are able to keep control of the clan they head.

The main benefit to followers of this adaptive leader is better rates of cub survival, which profits the species as a whole. Females are protected by the sisterhood from the aggressive advances of males when they are in heat. Their large communities are protective against other predators.

WHEN WOULD WE USE THE ADAPTIVE LEADERSHIP STYLE?

Spotted Hyenas are adaptive leaders in the way they have overcome things that held them back as a species. In 2011 the Boston Consulting Group conducted research on what adaptive leadership teams do differently or better than other teams who deliver average results. They interviewed more than 100 executive members of these teams in financial services, medical technology, chemicals, consumer goods, travel, hospitality, pharmaceuticals and private equity. According to Torres and Rimmer, who led the study, adaptive leaders should apply the following principles to be successful:

Share the leadership and develop up-and-coming leaders. Hyena hierarchal structure develops the next generation of leaders.
Set defined goals – today we are going to hunt zebra!
Develop mutual trust – if I go for the throat of the wildebeest, will you get the leg?

Who is suitable to this type of leadership?

Jeff Boss, writer for business magazine *Forbes*, identifies that adaptive thinkers need three characteristics:

- They need to have impulse control; be able to think before they act. That counts for hyena too – best not to tackle the prey unless you are pretty sure you can bring it down.
- Adaptive thinkers leave ego at the door. They show a willingness to let go of previous assumptions and experience.
- They are curious, willing to forgo the old and adopt new ways of doing things.

Being adaptive hyena-style is not a quick fix but a long-term approach to problem solving. What this style can teach us is that there is always another way of doing things. If at first you don't succeed, try something different. Think 'out of the box'. Be flexible and consider strategies that may seem way out there, and that no one else has tried – they may just work in your circumstances and in your environment.

IT'S HARD TO TELL MALE AND FEMALE HYENAS APART

According to an article by Matthew Blake, published in the *Daily Mail* in October 2014, a zoo in Japan tried for years to persuade their two Spotted Hyenas to breed. The animals, Kami and Kamutori, were thought to be a pair. The Maruyama Zoo in Sapporo found that Kami, now five years old, had never showed any oestrus signs after reaching sexual maturity. After years of waiting for the pitter-patter of little hyena paws, the zoo became worried. They decided to thoroughly examine both Kami and her six-year old partner Kamutori. Female hyenas are virtually indistinguishable from male hyenas. It turned out that in this case both animals had male genitalia. As both male and female parts look so similar in Spotted Hyenas, this was only discovered when both animals were examined very close up.

CHAPTER 6

THE LAISSEZ-FAIRE LEADER — AFRICAN LION

'A lioness has got a lot more power than
the lion likes to think she has.'

JACKI WEAVER

Lion.

King of the Beasts!

Portrayed in the legends of ancient Rome, Greece and Egypt and embodied in the traditions of African culture, the Lion is a symbol of royal leadership. In Egypt, the Lion gave form to the Sphinx and was engraved on Egyptian tombs. It was believed to act as a guide to the underworld, as suggested by the presence of lion-footed tombs and images of mummies being carried on the backs of Lions. But even earlier than this, Lion symbolism and iconography was widespread throughout Europe, Asia, and

Africa. Depictions of Lions are known from the Upper Paleolithic period. Paintings and carvings dating back 15,000 to 17,000 years were found in the Lascaux and Chauvet Caves in France, where Lions were portrayed as organised hunters with great strength and skill. Lions have remained popular symbols in modern times. In Chinese culture, costumed dancers still perform the lion dance, mimicking the movement of these big cats for good luck during Chinese New Year and the August Moon Festival. Lions are still depicted as mascots for sporting clubs, on family crests and as corporate or national symbols.

LAISSEZ-FAIRE LEADERSHIP – AFRICAN LION STYLE

Male African Lions have a typical laissez-faire leadership style, where the rights and power to make decisions are given to the worker. Females do 85 to 90 per cent of the pride's hunting, while the males often loaf about snoozing. A male is always the leader of the pride, however. One of the ways Lions defend the pride's territory is by scent marking to warn off intruders. Males and females mark their territory by spraying urine and scent from a gland at the base of the tail. This behaviour is so ingrained in cats that it can be difficult to stop a domestic cat from undertaking this 'service' in your house. Lions mark trees and bushes and scrape the ground whilst they are doing this in order to spread their scent around to let other lions know this territory is taken. Although the males are the protectors of the group, the females will also help to defend the pride against intruders.

The male is responsible for patrolling the territory and protecting the pride, for which they take the 'lion's share' of the females' prey. Although squabbling and fighting over food is common, adult males usually eat first, followed by the females and then the cubs. Females and cubs don't get to eat until after the male has had his fill. The male will however occasionally take on the larger prey such as buffalo and elephant.

Laissez-faire Lion leaders do not express their dominance over the pride overtly. They have a very laid-back attitude to leadership. Lions are often called the 'laziest' of the big cats. They may spend some sixteen to twenty hours a day sleeping and resting. When resting, Lions seem to enjoy good fellowship with lots of touching, head rubbing, licking and purring. But when it comes to food, each Lion looks out for itself.

There are usually only one or two adult male Lions in each pride. Very occasionally a coalition of three or even more males can be found in the one pride. Females spend their lives in their mothers' pride but if the group gets too big they can leave their birth place to find a new pride. There is no rank order amongst the lionesses but a female will often lead a hunting party even if a male is present. A male is always dominant with respect to food, though.

As in many mammal societies where a male is in charge of several females, the male Lions are considerably larger than females. This sexual dimorphism is very obvious in Lions. The male has a characteristic mane which the females lack. The mane was thought to help protect the male's neck during aggressive interactions with rival males. Dr Craig Packer, one of the world's leading lion researchers, believes that the mane may instead be a token of strength or status and conducted an intriguing experiment. He had a plush-toy company produce realistic life-size lions with different coloured manes of varying length. He called them Romeo, Fabio, Lothario and Julio. He enticed the real lions to the decoy lions with the calls of hyenas at a kill. Lions will often scare hyenas off their kill to steal their food. The lionesses were mostly attracted to the darker-haired manes. At the same time males avoided the dark-maned dummies.

Further research showed that many males with short manes had more injuries and illnesses, whilst darker-maned lions tended to be older and have higher testosterone levels. A lush, dark mane therefore seems to signal to females and other males that this male is strong and healthy. After observing Lions for several decades, Dr Packer believes that males establish a clear hierarchy within the pride. A dominant male usually sires most of the offspring. DNA testing has confirmed that this is the case. As females do most of the hunting, males can concentrate on mating to produce more cubs.

BRUISER THE AFRICAN LION

One of my favourite Lions is Bruiser, whom I have known since he was just a youngster. Louise Ginman, a Lion expert from Taronga Zoo, looked after Bruiser for many years and shares her stories about him in his younger days. Bruiser is now nineteen years old.

'One of my fondest memories is when Bruiser met his cubs for the first time when they were nine weeks old. Until then he had only met them though mesh, and now it was time for him to have full physical contact with them. It was the first litter for Kuchani, the cubs' mother, and she was an instinctive and protective parent. She always put herself between Bruiser and the cubs until she knew he wasn't going to hurt them. When one of the cubs walked underneath Bruiser's front legs, he literally jumped 1.5m (5ft) off the ground. He was just in absolute shock because he had no experience with cubs. It was so comical to see. He was the most gentle, wonderful father though. He let his cubs play with his mane, pull his tail and snuggle up with him. I'll never forget that first day though. The king of the jungle frightened of a little cub.

Bruiser is a respected leader, who understands give and take. A gentle leader. If the girls indicated for him to back away from them or something they had possession of, he would take note. Occasionally he showed he was a leader with privileges, though. If he really wanted something he had preferential rights to it. We had a beautiful lion toy for the pride, built to lion strength. It was a giant bungy toy, he could pull in a way that simulated bringing down prey. Nobody got near that toy when Bruiser was around as there was no way he would let anybody else touch it. The girls had to sit and wait. In the case of that toy, he gave the clear message: 'I am in charge of this family. I am the king of the family.' If it were a zebra the lionesses had hunted in the wilds of Africa, the message would have been exactly the same. Until he was exhausted and finished with the toy nobody else could touch it.'

LIFE IN THE PRIDE

Lions are the only social cat species, living in groups of related individuals and their offspring. Even if there is more than one male in the pride, one will be dominant over the others. Lionesses are very sociable; they hunt together, jointly defend their territory and even raise their cubs in a crèche. The size of a pride varies but the average is about fifteen individuals.

They can be active at any time but Lions are mostly nocturnal and crepuscular (active at dawn and dusk). Despite their long resting periods, activity peaks after dusk when there are likely to be spells during which most of the hunting occurs. Female Lions catch mostly small or medium-sized prey, such as warthog, gazelle, wildebeest or zebra. The males hunt the large prey such as buffalo and giraffe, where size and strength may be more important than speed.

When resting, the pride bond through head rubbing and licking, which has been compared with grooming in primates. Head rubbing against another Lion's forehead, face and neck seems to be used as a greeting. This is often seen in domestic cats too when their humans come home. Males head-rub other males in the pride and females and cubs head-rub other females. Lions are most affectionate to their same-sex companions. Social licking happens at the same time, with the head and neck being the most common areas. It is handy to have that help provided by pride members as these bits of the body can't be reached by the cat itself and they tend to become dirty through feeding on messy carcasses.

Most of the images and documentaries we see about lions show a group of females bringing down a zebra or a springbok. Lions hunt cooperatively when the prey is large or difficult to bring down. When the prey can be caught by one individual, the other Lions will hold back and watch until the kill is made. Lions stalk their prey from a distance and move slowly and carefully so as to be undetected until they are close enough to make the final charge, often from a distance of less than 50m (165ft). Once captured, the Lion bites the snout or throat to kill.

Once the prey is killed, the guts are eaten first as hides are tough to breach and the skin on the belly is easier to tear. They then make a start on the fleshy parts. Other pride members who arrive have to tackle the thick hides or wait until they can find a spot in the feeding frenzy.

When females are in season it is a busy time for Lions. Females are polyestrous, meaning that they cycle throughout the year, and heat lasts about four days. During Lion mating time in Taronga Zoo, quietly working in my office, I would often hear the roars of a mating pair ringing out across the zoo. They can potentially mate every 15 minutes for four days straight. Quite a feat. No wonder the females do most of the hunting – the males are probably either too busy or too tired. The constant calls of mating Lions when you are trying to work can be a tad distracting though!

LION CUBS LEARN THROUGH PLAY

In zoos, cubs are handled by zookeepers for a period of time to reduce the potential stress of future veterinary procedures, such as vaccinations. Three Lion cubs at Taronga Zoo were handled regularly. We frequently assessed if it was still safe to do so whilst the cubs grew. Lions are great stalkers and when they kill they often use suffocation. One Lion gets a good grab of the victim's throat or neck and crushes the windpipe. Alternatively they clamp their mouth over the prey's nose and mouth whilst the other Lions hold it down.

When the cubs at Taronga Zoo were five months old, I had not been to visit them for a few weeks due to a vacation. When I sat down in their den area, as I had done before, I realised how much they had grown over the time I'd been away. They'd obviously been practicing their hunting skills for a while.

As I was playing with them, a bit like you would a kitten, they decided to practice their cooperative hunting skills. Two cubs kept me occupied at the front, while the other one went for my neck. They weighed close to 20kg (44lb) by then and their size and newly developed skills showed that they were now too big to play with us.

Fortunately, I survived.

MALE COMPETITION FOR THE ALPHA JOB

Male Lions leave or get pushed out of their birth pride some time between two and four years of age. They leave the pride together with other young males and form groups or coalitions. During this time, the males are nomadic whilst they grow to full maturity.

Once they reach maturity, they will try to establish their own prides by attempting to overthrow the male or males of another pride. If they are able to replace a pride's males, they will kill all the pride's cubs.

This happens because they want to produce their own offspring and the females will not come into season whilst they have young cubs. Females come into season again once their cubs are almost two years of age. If a female's cubs are killed though she will mate again within days. A male may only be able to hold the alpha position in a pride for a few years before he, too, is ousted by a challenging male. So he can't wait for another male's cubs to grow up if he wants to pass on his own genes. It is estimated that infanticide may responsible for a quarter of all lion cub deaths. Louise Ginman comments:

'Raising cubs is really costly for lionesses. They are pregnant for four months, then feed and raise the cubs for up to another eighteen months. It is because of this huge maternal investment that the role of the male is really important to the lionesses. Ideally there is more than one male, a coalition of brothers is common, of which one is the dominant male. They protect the females from unfamiliar males taking over the group and killing the cubs. Lionesses prefer the strongest, most confident male to sire their offspring – the best genes to pass on.'

Given that a male has a harem of females with whom he mates, and that birth-rates are 50 per cent male and 50 per cent female, there are a lot of males who never get to join a pride as an alpha male. The top job in a pride is challenging and takes a toll on the leader. To make sure his genetic lineage gets passed on he has to constantly fight off other males. It has been observed that lionesses, on occasion, will support the alpha male in helping to attack the challenging male. The females are obviously invested in their cubs surviving. If a new male does succeed in taking over the leadership of the pride the adolescent males and females may be expelled from the pride. Although the adolescents escape infanticide, life outside an established pride is tough and starvation a significant risk.

LIONESSES IN THE PRIDE

Lionesses have agility and speed on their side. Evolution has favoured them to be a near-perfect predator – strong enough to bring down a mighty wildebeest but fast enough to catch a gazelle. Their sandy coat blends in beautifully with the savanna grasses and their hunting coalitions increase their kill rate.

Lionesses are a stable element in the pride. They are loyal and supportive to other pride members but don't tolerate outsider females. A study in Tanzania over three decades suggests that females do not establish a hierarchy amongst themselves. According to Dr Packer, females in a pride form a community in which all the females are of the same social standing. The social equality of female Lions is very different from the behaviour of wolves and many other species where an alpha female is the only one to breed. This equality in lionesses is unusual in social species.

They also work together to rear their young. The cubs are placed in a crèche and cared for cooperatively.

No one is boss and everyone contributes. There are significant advantages in such a society. Lionesses who give birth around the same time seek each other out. When mothers are away hunting they need competent and trustworthy babysitters. Cooperation benefits all parties. Each female minding the cub nursery is prepared to defend them as she too has a stake in cub survival. Female Lions are known to kill the cubs of rival prides, but they never kill the cubs of their own pride. Adult female membership tends to only change with the births and deaths of lionesses.

WHAT CAN WE LEARN FROM LION LAISSEZ-FAIRE LEADERSHIP?

Laissez-faire leaders will ensure that the team knows what their goals are and then lets them get on with it without micromanaging their daily activities. They will often set the parameters of what needs to be accomplished (hunt prey!) and a self-managed team of lionesses will complete the task. If the team is well-trained and motivated they are likely to need very little control and supervision. In such cases, a good laissez-faire management style will give little guidance and still produce great results.

The benefits of this leadership style for lions is that the leader gives power and freedom to his followers. The alpha expects the team to solve problems, make decisions and gives little day-to-day direction.

WHAT DO LION FOLLOWERS EXPECT FROM THEIR LAISSEZ-FAIRE LEADER?

In nature, animals will often choose their leader by attaching themselves to another group with an effective leader. Lionesses can't easily attach themselves to a new pride. New females are not accepted in another established pride. Their choices are to either support their leader during a challenge or not support him.

The lionesses do most of the work hunting the food for the pride. What, then, can the male contribute to their lives that makes him earn his keep? His main job is to make babies. As the strongest, healthiest male around, his genes are worth propagating. Important too is his role as the protector of the group, shielding the lionesses and their offspring from any danger, particularly the advances of rival males where take-overs would result in the death of their cubs. Male Lions are also the ones to take on the bigger prey such as elephants and buffalo. Additionally the females benefit from this leadership style because they have the ability to apply their skills, make most of their own decisions and have equality in the female coalition.

WHEN WOULD WE USE THE LAISSEZ-FAIRE LEADERSHIP STYLE?

From my observations of social animals, the laissez-faire leadership style can work in some situations and with some teams. This style is also known as a 'delegative' leadership. Leaders are mostly laid-back and permit group members make their own decisions. This leadership style can also lead to low productivity. In view of the male Lion's sexual activities, however, it is obviously a leadership style that gives him time to engage productively in his core business, namely reproductively engaging with the females in his harem.

As with all types of leadership, there are both pros and cons to this style. In a team of experts, particularly if their expertise is not shared by the leader, this style can work well. The team must have the skills and ability to work independently and complete the task with very little guidance. Such a team may appreciate the freedom to work relatively independently and are likely to have sufficient motivation to succeed. The leader should still be available to ensure the team has all the tools it needs to be successful, to offer feedback and to assist where needed – as in capture the big prey such as elephants, or whatever your business equivalent of 'elephants' might be.

This style does not suit a situation where the team members lack the skills or experience to make the necessary decisions and to accomplish their mission. Lions would not send out the inexperienced adolescents on their own without the guidance and support of more capable pride members. In an inexperienced team, members may not understand their role or responsibilities well enough to use their time effectively. The leader needs to set clear goals and timelines for achieving key outcomes and communicate these regularly. A laissez-faire leader with an inexperienced staff or a team that is somewhat dysfunctional could see projects falling off the rails and deadlines missed, leading to low job satisfaction for all involved.

The laissez-faire leader may give the impression that they are not involved with the team or are avoiding the leadership role. Such a leader may even blame the team if the desired results are not achieved. This may be a person promoted for their technical skills, with little management experience who has not led teams before. They may need to learn how to provide leadership for their team as they grow more comfortable in the new role.

However, the laissez-faire style is suited very well to leaders who are naturally more laid-back than others. They should be aware, however, that when leading a team that lacks depth or experience they may need to switch to a more hands-on manner until the group develops the ability to work more independently.

Back to our Lion example... In summary, the alpha Lion gives freedom and agency to the pride. This works well when the pride is highly skilled and experienced. In return, the pride can count on the leader to help out when needed and for important matters, such as ensuring the survival of the pride. Good leaders take care of those in his or her charge and make them feel protected.

LIONS ON THE RED LIST

According to the IUCN Red List of Threatened Species the African Lion population is considered to have decreased by 43 per cent over 21 years (1993-2014). The causes of decline are the killing of Lions to protect humans and livestock, loss of habitat and the decreased availability of prey. The decreasing food supply is linked to habitat loss, poaching and the bushmeat trade. An emerging threat is the use of bones and other body parts in traditional medicine. Trophy hunting also has a significant impact on the long-term survival of Lions in Africa. The largest males with the biggest manes are targeted as hunting trophies. They are also likely to be the alpha male in a pride. With the removal of that male a new male, or a coalition of new males, will take over the control of the pride. The new males will kill all the cubs to bring the females into season quickly. Cubs take two years to become independent. If the frequency of leadership change increases, the pride does not have the ability to sustain itself. Although trophy hunting *claims* it has a positive impact in some areas, contributing funds for conservation efforts in Africa, it appears to have contributed to the decline of Lion numbers in Botswana, Namibia, Tanzania, Zimbabwe, Cameroon and Zambia. Conservationists constantly call for the better regulation of trophy hunting to ensure sustainability – with varying degrees of success.

CHAPTER 7

THE DEMOCRATIC LEADER

*'Democracy must be something more than two wolves
and a sheep voting on what to have for dinner.'*

JAMES BOVARD

Nature is inherently undemocratic and violent, right?

The popular perception is that the natural world is ruled by aggression and through the domination of others. However, in my experience, wherever violence and domination exist in the animal world, so do aspects of democracy and shared decision making. Democracy is not a construct of human culture alone. Research into how choices and decisions are made in the animal world clearly demonstrates that many animal societies have some democratic processes. However, whereas a silverback gorilla is a credible example of an authoritarian leader and a male Lion of a laissez-faire leader, it is harder to find a true poster child for democracy in the animal world.

Nevertheless, democratic principles such as voting and collective decision-making have been observed in African Buffaloes, Red Deer, pigeons, bees, baboons and many more species. Lixing Sun and colleagues studied Tibetan Macaques to understand how a group of twelve of these monkeys coordinated their travels. They noticed that once three or more of them moved together the entire group would be likely to follow. The success rate in getting the group moving got better and better as the number of supporters increased. By the time seven or more macaques were ready to go a majority had been formed and the success rate reached its maximum 100 per cent.

The data from research into democracy in animals is increasing our understanding of how this works in nature, suggesting that the principle of democracy in humans seems to have a clear biological origin. The majority rule in decision-making, even in hierarchical societies, safeguards the will of most of the individuals in the group. It seems to be the best way in nature to avoid or resolve conflict in social beings, whether it's a troop of baboons or a swarm of Honey Bees. It is no wonder then that humans use the same model to make important decisions such as electing the next President, although in our case having the right knowledge to make a good decision would be an advantage.

DEMOCRATIC LEADERSHIP STYLE

Democratic leadership allows individuals who may be considered subordinate by hierarchal standards to have shared power in making decisions. Democratic leaders value collaboration and the free-flow of ideas. Variations of democratic decision-making can be seen in many animal societies. If we live together because there are benefits in doing so, we have to try to minimise the number of things we might argue over. In mammalian societies with a clear hierarchy, such as those of monkeys or deer, there is a dominant individual who rules all others. Tim Roper, from the University of Kent, says that many researchers have simply assumed that this dictator also makes the decisions, such as where to go or how long to feed for. Although a dominant leading male may keep all breeding rights for himself, it now seems that he does not necessarily decide on everything else.

Male dominance in animal societies nearly always has to do with sex. Access to the females in order to maximise numbers of offspring is priority number one. Access to food is important too but not always as high a priority as sex. Being a dominant male is quite stressful. Leaving some room for decisions about foraging to be made by other group members makes a lot of sense. It helps to keep the peace and requires less involvement from the leader. On the other hand, female dominance nearly always has to do with access to food so that her offspring may thrive. It is for this reason that older females are likely to be followed by others in their preferred direction for finding food.

Many hierarchical societies employ some aspects of democracy once ranking within the group is settled. The scientific literature when reporting on shared decision-making will often study how the decision to move and the direction of travel is reached. This is such an important decision that is taken daily or even several times per day by animal groups. It is also an activity that can be studied by researchers in the wild. The wrong decision can mean no food or a predator waiting. Given the importance of that decision, it is perhaps even more surprising to discover that the most common research finding shows animal communities voting for their preferred option.

Finding a way of making shared decisions stabilises social organisations. Animals may choose between two mutually exclusive actions. Shall we go west or shall we go south? In the case of people, we know how that works. A consensus decision is when all group members feel they have an opportunity to contribute equally to the decision. Sharing the decision-making is more effective than a group accepting the decision of a single dominant member. According to research by biologists Larissa Conradt and Tim Roper, groups are less impulsive: 'Democratic decisions are more beneficial primarily because they tend to produce less extreme decisions, because each individual has an influence on the decision per se.'

The Red Deer of Eurasia live in large herds, spending lots of time either grazing or lying down to ruminate. Some deer are ready to move on before others are. Scientists have noticed that herds only move when 60 per cent of the adults stand up, literally voting with their feet. Even if an individual is more dominant than others in the group, herds typically favour democratic decisions over autocratic ones.

DEMOCRATIC DECISION MAKING
IN A HIERARCHICAL SOCIETY

There was a time in the 1960s when anthropologists thought that baboons, rather than apes, were perhaps our closest relatives. Olive Baboons live in complex social societies. They are adapted to the environmental circumstances that our ancestors would have encountered after coming down from the trees. They hunt communally on open grassland, while an alpha male leads the troop and keeps the females in line, just like our human ancestors. Since that time, more field observations of the baboons and the advances of DNA analysis have changed our categorisation of baboons.

We now know that apes are our closest relatives. Where baboons are *not* similar to humans is when they hunt. Olive Baboons seem to have disorganised hunts described as a 'free-for-all' by baboon researcher Robert Sapolsky in his book *A Primate's Memoir*. He adds: 'The alpha male couldn't lead the troop to food during a crisis as he would not know where to go.' Males transfer into the group as adolescents, while females are philopatric, spending their entire life in the troop they are born into. 'Thus, it would be the old females who remembered the grove of olive trees past the fourth hill.' The group was therefore more likely to trust an older female to remember where food could be found.

Conflicts of interest about where to go and what to do are a primary challenge of group living. Tracking wild Olive Baboons with a high-resolution Global Positioning System (GPS) and analysing their movements relative to one another reveals that a process of shared decision-making governs their movement too. Rather than preferentially following dominant individuals, Olive

Baboons are more likely to follow when one baboon initiates the direction of travel and several troop members agree.

One would expect that, with hierarchical social structures such as those found in many primates, democracy may be complicated by dominance. Strandburg-Peshkin *et al.* monitored all the individuals within a baboon troop continuously over the course of their daily activities. Within this highly socially structured species, movement decisions come about via a shared process. Demonstrating that evolutionarily, democracy may be an inherent trait in a variety of primate species.

The study, led by researchers from Smithsonian Tropical Research Institute, Oxford University and Princeton University, simultaneously tracked members of a troop of baboons with GPS trackers. Despite the strong pecking order in the troop, the study found that all individuals potentially have a say over where the troop goes, including those with low social status. The study also discovered that females have as much influence on troop movements as the more dominant males.

Twenty-five wild baboons in Kenya were fitted with GPS collars that recorded each individual's location once per second for a fortnight. These GPS data points showed exactly how each baboon moved relative to another. Movement patterns showed that animals with higher rank did not have a greater chance of attracting followers.

Whenever conflicts about direction arose, the group had two solutions to resolve the problem:

1. If the difference between the directions was less than 90 degrees, the group would compromise by taking a 'middle way'.

When the difference was greater than 90 degrees they would go with the majority decision. This suggests that baboons use similar movement rules to many other animals, such as fish and birds.

'It seems that, despite their complex social structure, when it comes to disagreements over where to move it's a case of 'one baboon, one vote' as decision-making is largely a shared, 'democratic' process,' says Dr Damien Farine of Oxford University. 'Patterns of collective movement in baboons are remarkably similar to models that can predict the movements of fish, birds, and insects, which use a simple set of rules such as 'follow your neighbour'.'

This research shows an important distinction between social status and leadership and demonstrates that democratic decision-making can work well even in socially stratified societies.

AFRICAN BUFFALO AND DEMOCRATIC DECISION MAKING

African Buffalo are herd-living vegetarians. They too make group decisions about when and where to move. In the 1990s, Herbert Prins realised that what initially looked like 'mundane stretching' was actually a type of 'voting behaviour,' in which females indicate their travel preferences by standing up, staring in one direction and then lying back down.

'Only adult females vote, and females participate regardless of their social status within the herd. Some buffalo cows arise, shuffle around a bit and bed down again. At first, I interpreted this as 'stretching the legs,' but one day I noticed that the cows adopt a particular stance after the shuffling and before lying down again. They seem to gaze in one direction and keep their head higher than the normal resting position but lower than the alert... This standing up, gazing and lying down behaviour continues for about an hour, but the overall impression remains that of a herd totally at rest. Then at about 18.00 hours there is a sudden energising of the herd... A few moments later, everywhere in the herd buffalo start trekking. The exciting thing is that they start trekking, at the beginning independently of each other, in the same direction. Within seconds, the animals that initiate these movements are followed by other individuals, clusters of movement arise, and within about three to five minutes the whole herd of hundreds of individuals moves as if conducted by one master. They totally give the impression that they know where they are going to: apparently, some decision has been taken in the group.'

There are days when the cows have different opinions on where to graze. When that happens the herd may split and graze on different patches for the night.

Animal groups that move as a unit have to come up with some way of deciding how decisions are to be made. Many have a similar strategy, using sounds, body posture, looking in a certain direction or even sneezing to vote for a particular action, as seen in African Wild Dogs.

MORE ABOUT ANIMALS VOTING

Pigeons rarely get respect on city streets, but according to biologists, Paulo Jorge and Paulo Marques at Oxford University, they have complex social hierarchies in which even low-ranking birds can vote on the flock's next flight. Using GPS trackers attached to tiny backpacks, the researchers found that: 'Most birds have a say in decision-making, a flexible system of 'rank' ensures that some birds are more likely to lead and others to follow.' This kind of set-up, they add: 'May represent a particularly efficient form of decision-making.'

In 2003, Larissa Conradt and Tim Roper, in the journal *Nature*, modelled differences in decision making between 'despotic' animal leaders and 'democratic' animal leaders. They suggest that under most conditions, the costs to subordinate group members, and to the group as a whole, are considerably higher for despotic leadership than for democratic decisions. Even when the despot is the most experienced group member, it only pays other members to accept his or her decision when group size is small and the difference in information is large.

WHAT CAN WE LEARN FROM DEMOCRATIC ANIMAL LEADERSHIP?

Democracy and voting by animals are not subjects that have been studied to any great degree as yet. In most cases we know more about dominance in animals than we do about democracy. As studies progress, we are likely to find that there are a great many more species that use democracy as a key component of group living. The core principle of democracy, however, appears to have a biological origin judging by the frequency with which it is found in nature. The simple 'majority rule' seems to be a good way of avoiding or resolving conflicting interests in animals or people that live or work in communal societies. The prevalence of shared decision-making in such a diverse range of social animal species, from pigeons to cockroaches, suggests an evolutionary need for it and that it helps a species to thrive.

Even when there are hierarchies and leaders, the democratic systems allow for input from other members of the community. In animal groups, this leadership style suits a dynamic and rapidly changing environment. In complex, fast-moving organisations, this can help the group stay up-to-date with all the latest developments in their industry. Democratic leadership offers flexibility to quickly change to alternative ways of doing things. The democratic leader follows a collegial style of running a team and is a consensus builder. Ideas can be shared amongst the group with everyone having a seat at the table. Discussion can be open and free-flowing.

This style in animal communities benefits both the leader and the followers. The leader shares the responsibility for decisions that affect the whole group and has the confidence to accept that others in the group have particular skills and knowledge that can lead to better outcomes for all. Some older animals may have better knowledge of where food is plentiful at the moment. The downside is that democracy can be slow. Decision-making processes can become protracted with extensive consultation and stakeholder involvement. Generally, however, democratic leaders bring the best out of an experienced and expert team. Followers feel empowered to use their combined skills and talents, and sharing ideas and views allows for continued learning on the job. People feel valued for their expertise, rather than simply obliged to follow orders from less-informed superiors. This leadership style brings people together as equals.

WHAT DO FOLLOWERS EXPECT FROM THEIR DEMOCRATIC LEADER?

Animal leaders with some democratic aspects to their leadership are likely to inspire trust and respect amongst their followers. Those leaders are confident enough to allow others to suggest the next course of action. The main benefit to teams under this leadership style is that shared decision-making prevents and resolves conflict without aggression or dominance from the leader. The entire community prospers as group harmony and cohesion are preserved. This style brings a certain social equality that followers of autocratic leaders do not have. The interests of the group are represented and persuasive animals that influence the decisions are validated for their knowledge. The entire community benefits as the group has ownership of the decisions that affect their future.

WHEN WOULD WE USE THE DEMOCRATIC LEADERSHIP STYLE?

While democratic leadership is a very effective leadership style, it does have some potential drawbacks. For this leadership style to work well, the team needs to have skilled members who really have something valuable to share. Roles and boundaries need to be clear and the project must allow time for the consultation process. Democratic leadership can lead to communication failures and uncompleted projects if the skill-base does not allow for contributions of high quality. Conversely, if skilled people have their ideas ignored, they can feel like their input is mere lip-service and this can lead to low job satisfaction. Democratic leadership works best when group members are capable and keen to share their ideas. This style also contributes to good social cohesion in the team.

The fact that democratic traits have evolved in numerous and diverse animal species demonstrates that, in nature, there are many benefits to using democratic decision-making. Research in humans has found that this leadership style is one of the most effective and creates higher morale and productivity. It can result in more creative solutions to problems because all group members are encouraged to participate and share their thoughts and ideas. The democratic leader is still there to offer guidance and some control if needed, but the focus is on equality in the group.

CHAPTER 8

THE MATERNALISTIC LEADER – ELEPHANT

'The Indian Elephant is said sometimes to weep'

CHARLES DARWIN

In popular thinking, elephants represent strength, wisdom, longevity, leadership and loyalty. They have a harmonious social organisation with close family ties. Elephants form lifelong friendships, act out of loyalty, show compassion and mourn their dead. Elephantidae is the only surviving family of the order Proboscidea, whose other members included the mammoths and mastodons (giant elephant-like animals), which are now extinct.

The African Savanna Elephant, the African Forest Elephant and the Asian Elephant are large-brained intelligent animals. African and Asian Elephants diverged some six million years ago but fulfil a similar role in their respective environments. Both are large, generalist plant-eaters. Asian Elephants have worked with humans for thousands of years in forestry, hunting and even warfare. They have carried royalty and now, sadly, are called upon to carry tourists in many countries. The African Elephant is considered to be harder to train than the Asian Elephant but they, too, have worked for humans, mostly during wartime. Hannibal's army travelled across the Alps with African Elephants to attack the Romans in 200 BC and elephant populations in North Africa were the source of war elephants. War elephants were first used in India and the practice spread across South-East Asia and westwards to the Mediterranean. Their most famous use was during the Pyrrhic War (280–275 BC) in Roman Italy. The ancient Romans, Carthaginians and Ethiopians all collected elephants for their war activities. The African Elephant disappeared from north of the Sahara by around the 6th century AD.

MATERNALISTIC LEADERSHIP – ELEPHANT STYLE

Elephants are the largest living terrestrial mammal and live in matriarchal societies. The herd is made up of related females with young, occasionally followed on the periphery by a couple of males looking for an opportunity to mate.

They are a great example of the maternalistic leadership style. A maternalistic leader looks after her family as a wise mother or a grandmother would. Leading them to food and water and protecting them against predators. The females are ranked by age and possibly by personality. There is no overt competition for the top job. The alpha position in African Elephants mostly goes to the matriarch's oldest daughter after her death or when she's no longer up to the leadership position. Age and life experience are the most valued attributes for an alpha female elephant. These older females are a critical resource in a group of long-lived social mammals. Studies show that she can remember a severe drought of twenty or thirty years ago and knows where to lead the herd to water and food if this happens again. When the herd follows their leader to water, the waterhole could be days away. The matriarch knows where she is going and the rest of the herd follows on the basis of trust.

There is a difference in the matriarchal systems between African and Asian Elephants but some of the leadership traits are common to both. African Elephants live in bigger herds and it is in their best interest to have a leader they can all gravitate to in times of crisis. Africa also has more unpredictability in the environment, such as extended periods of drought, and the herd may have to travel long distances to find food and water. Nearly all seasonal movements have a similar pattern – a mass migration from permanent water holes once the rainy season starts, followed by a return to permanent water at the end of the rains, when the temporary water holes dry up. This movement relies on a matriarch knowing where to go. It is easy to see who the matriarch is in African Elephants as they all cluster around that one female.

The social structure of Asian Elephants is a bit different to that of African Elephants as their environment is more predictable. Asian Elephants live in smaller herds and herd structure is looser and more flexible with elephants joining and separating from the herd frequently. Despite its long association with humans, there are fewer scientific studies on the social structure of the Asian Elephant in the wild, compared with African Elephants. In Asian Elephant groups it is less obvious who the matriarch is as individuals move in and out of the group more frequently than in the herds of their African counterparts. Only a crisis will unquestionably confirm the Asian Elephant matriarch, when members of the group will gather around her.

DO ELEPHANTS GRIEVE?

Elephants are known to be intelligent, emotional animals. If an elephant comes across the bones of another elephant, it will be quiet and respectful. Its body posture will change: the tail and ears may droop. They will pick up the bones and roll them around on the ground. The bones of other large animals are not handled in this way - only elephant bones. They are reported to come back to the spot where a herd member died and may continue to pay their respects for years. There are also reports of elephants covering another elephant who has died with branches and dirt. Some elephants have broken into research camps to take a bone back from scientists and return it to the spot of that elephant's demise.

HOW ELEPHANT SOCIETY WORKS

Asian and African Elephant families revolve around females

and their young. They raise their calves with the help of their grandmothers, mothers, aunts and sisters. The flexible group structure means that they are not together all the time, something we see in other mammal groups, such as chimpanzees and hyenas too. Sometimes several family groups join up and form slightly less stable associations which are called 'clans' or 'kinship groups'.

Elephant clan members communicate through touch, sight, smell and sound. The sounds include chirps, loud trumpeting and low-frequency rumbles, which are undetectable to our ears. They also use body language such as a flap of the ears, a shake of the head, kicks and nudges. Over long distances they use infrasound and seismic communication. Infrasound, also called low-frequency sound, is lower in frequency than 20 Hertz or 20 cycles-per-second, which is the lower limit of human hearing. Infrasonic calls are important in both Asian and African Elephants, particularly for long-distance communication. Elephants are also known to communicate through seismic vibrations produced by impacts on the ground or the sound waves that travel through it. They appear to use their leg and shoulder bones to transmit the signals to the middle ear. When detecting seismic signals, the animals lean forward and put more weight on their larger front feet; this is known as 'freezing behaviour'.

Observations by Karen McCombe and others in Amboseli National Park in Kenya showed the benefits of older matriarchs leading family groups. The research group played recordings of male and female Lions roaring – the matriarchs showed greater sensitivity to the roaring of males (which are larger, stronger and more likely to attack elephants) than lionesses. Over a period of many years the experience of hearing Lions call gives older females an advantage over the younger ones. Older matriarchs were able to detect the presence of male Lions at an earlier stage than the younger elephants. This resulted in the group 'bunching' close together creating a snug circle around the calves, ready to defend them. The study also concluded that elephant matriarchs can make important distinctions between different threat levels, distinguishing between the potential threats of female versus male Lions as predators. The accumulated knowledge of the older female influences how the group prepares for a possible predator attack and highlights the role of the older matriarch plays in her family.

Successful elephant matriarchs are not self-appointed leaders, rather, they are chosen by their family because they are respected. Respect comes from years of demonstrating that they can be trusted to make good decisions during a crisis.

THE MALE ELEPHANTS' WAY OF LIFE

From a young age, male elephants like to hang out with other males and play-fight. As they play they begin to test their strength and learn the fighting skills they need as older males. I have vivid memories of watching five young bulls play-fighting together at a waterhole in Etosha National Park, Namibia. I watched them for hours on end as they played, pushing and shoving each other into the water, jumping on top of each other. They were having a ball until a fearless Honey Badger came around. The Honey Badger, a rough diamond amongst the animals of Africa, literally scared the living daylights out of them. The bulls ran from the waterhole to get away, trumpeting loudly. The Honey Badger seemed to just enjoy scattering these big beasts – quite a feat for a small carnivore weighing between 7–13kg (15–30lb). The Honey Badger is known for its aggression and feared by many other animals in its environment.

Male elephants, known as bulls, have very different social needs than females. In the wild, males leave or are driven out of the family group by the older females when they reach puberty. By the age of 25, males are twice the size of females. They may join or form bachelor groups once they leave the maternal herd. Bachelor elephants can be quite sociable when they are not competing for dominance or females, and they form long-term friendships. Caitlin O'Connell-Rodwella, an elephant researcher, relates the following stories about male elephants:

'They have a reputation as loners. But in Amboseli National Park in Kenya, where the longest-running studies on male elephants have been conducted, bulls have been observed to have a best friend with whom they associate for years. Another study, in Botswana, found that younger males seek out older males and learn social behaviours from them. In my previous field seasons at Mushara, I'd noticed that males had not just one close buddy but several, and that these large groups of males of mixed ages persisted for many years. Of the 150 bulls that we were monitoring, the group I was particularly interested in, which I called 'The Boys' Club' comprised up to fifteen individuals – a dominant bull and his entourage. Bulls of all ages appeared remarkably close, physically demonstrating their friendship.'

A dominance hierarchy exists among the males, when they hang out in a group. Dominance depends on age, size and sexual condition. When they are in groups, males follow the lead of the dominant bull. The company and leadership of older and more experienced males appear to control the aggression of the younger bulls. Adult males and females only come together for reproduction. The bulls stay close to family groups when there is a cow in season.

Female elephants continue to have influence over males even if they are far away. The increasing human population is forcing Asian Elephants in Sri Lanka into smaller and smaller feeding areas. This has led to male elephants in particular venturing onto farms and raiding farmers' crops. An elephant can destroy a farmer's crop in a matter of minutes, leaving the family with no income. A study by Wijayagunawardane and colleagues has found that if a sound recording of a female herd was played, the males abandoned their crop-raiding and fled into the forest. This finding suggests that farmers could potentially use these recordings to protect their crops, but it also highlights the respect male elephants have for the female herds.

SPECIAL ELEPHANT SENSES

Elephants are considered to have amazing senses and experience the world through smell and hearing much more than they do through sight. A study in Namibia tracked wild elephants fitted with GPS radio collars. The study found that the elephants living in this arid part of the world were able to detect thunderstorms days before the rains actually happened. They would show this by changing their direction of travel towards the expected rains. One way this can be explained is that elephants hear infrasound. These soundwaves are well below what humans can hear. Infrasound is used by elephants to communicate with each other over long distances. It is possible that they can also hear thunder many miles away.

STEPPING UP TO LEAD

The elephant herd I know best is the one at Taronga Zoo in Sydney. The Taronga Asian Elephant herd was put together from individual elephants used in the tourist trade in Thailand. Whereas the normal herd structure for Asian Elephants would be a mother, her offspring and perhaps their offspring, the Taronga herd came together in a more simulated way. Senior elephant keeper Lucy Melo shares her memories of that time:

'We had our original four females from Thailand and a young male called Gung. When we put these five strangers together to form a herd we knew who was going to be the leader. Porntip emerged as the 'matriarch' because of her personality. She was compassionate and knowledgeable; had that wisdom about her. Porntip was also the oldest in the group so that gave her more street-cred. Very soon all the elephants were following her around. She did not always love that but the group clearly wanted to be close to her. These elephants had not had the opportunity to be in a herd structure previously. Before they came to us they were used to being alone and chained to a tree all day long. So having this group structure was really different for them and they showed they liked it. They had a leader in Porntip and chose to be near her.'

Porntip showed her willingness to be the leader the group needed. Lucy adds:

'Porntip took her role very seriously. In the first week they were in Sydney a peacock landed in the elephant yard. It was the scariest thing these elephants had experienced! The first thing the whole group did was run to Porntip. All freaked out, they clumped together huddling in a protective circle. Porntip was the one to face the peacock. She must have thought: 'Well, I'm the matriarch so I have to do something about this.' She was the one who ventured out from that cluster of elephants, ears flapping and running towards the scary intruder to shoo him away. That's how a matriarch earns the respect of her followers.'

Another way in which Porntip demonstrated her care for the group was at night. The elephant sleeping area has cameras so that keepers can watch the group and Lucy saw the following scenario each morning as she reviewed the recordings:

'Porntip was always, always, always the last elephant to bed down. She would be the one standing up, maybe dozing on her feet occasionally, but standing up. It would take her a long time before she made the commitment to lay down too. Not until she considered everyone safe and asleep she would lay down herself. That goes to show that there is a luxury in *not* being the matriarch. You don't have to worry so much.'

Porntip was only twelve years old when she started to fulfil the role of matriarch and was therefore very young, in elephant years, for the responsibilities that came with the job. However, she was the eldest in the group, illustrating that in the absence of a leader, some elephants will step up and take responsibility, in the same way that humans do.

WHAT CAN WE LEARN FROM ELEPHANT MATERNALISTIC LEADERSHIP?

Leadership is important in coordinating family life in an elephant society. But what can we learn from the way an elephant matriarch advances the wellbeing of the group? She has qualities that are of substantial value to the team, qualities that will help the team to thrive. She is brave and protects; she is compassionate and nurturing; but above all she is intelligent and has life experience. Studies on elephants have demonstrated that the decision-making of the leader can benefit the group in several ways. For instance, by being aware of an approaching predator and taking immediate action to prevent an attack. The life experience, or corporate knowledge, of a leader is highly relevant in elephant societies where the matriarch plays a key role in organising the activities of the group.

The knowledge gained over a lifetime of experiences is recognised in many human societies, although certain cultures prize it more highly than others. Young people in western societies are often inclined to dismiss older experienced personnel, due to the rapid changes in technology and the workplace. Western culture is also one that values the 'young and beautiful' more highly than age and experience. The contribution by older and possibly wiser leaders and workers should not be overlooked. In humans a paternalistic or maternalistic leader works by applying the dynamics of family to their group, particularly with reference to giving guidance based on experience and nurturing their followers as a parent would.

MAJOR THREATS TO ELEPHANTS

The IUCN Red List of Threatened Species reports the following threats to elephants:

'African Elephant – Poaching for ivory and meat has traditionally been the major cause of the species' decline. Although illegal hunting remains a significant factor in some areas, particularly in Central Africa, currently the most important perceived threat is the loss and fragmentation of habitat caused by ongoing human population growth and rapid land conversion. A specific manifestation of this trend is the reported increase in human-elephant conflict, which further aggravates the threat to elephant populations.'

'Asian Elephant – The pre-eminent threats to the Asian Elephant today are habitat loss, degradation and fragmentation, which are driven by human population growth. There are increasing conflicts between humans and elephants when elephants eat or trample crops. Hundreds of people and elephants are killed annually as a result of such conflicts. The long-term future of elephants outside protected areas, as well as in some protected areas, is therefore linked to mitigating such human-elephant conflicts, and this is one of the largest conservation challenges in Asia today. Poaching is a major threat to elephants in Asia too, although reliable estimates of the number of elephants killed and the quantities of ivory and other body parts collected and traded are scarce.'

WHAT DO ELEPHANT FOLLOWERS EXPECT FROM THEIR MATERNALISTIC LEADER?

In the matriarch, elephant followers have a leader they can trust. She can be counted on to protect them from any danger. She will share her knowledge with the group and train the next generation. The matriarch, with the help of others, will keep aggressive males at bay. She protects the young in the herd against predation. The followers trust that the matriarch's experience will lead them to food, water, and resting places when they need them. They also benefit from having a leader who cares about them and their wellbeing as individuals and will do everything in her power to ensure the family thrives.

WHEN WOULD WE USE THE MATERNALISTIC LEADERSHIP STYLE?

Under what circumstances would this type of leadership suit our modern society? Modern leadership literature claims that workers under this style of leadership are expected to be completely committed to the organisation, the leader and what the leader believes. This could be considered an advantage as the leader intends all followers to succeed, potentially resulting in less competition for attention and resources in teams. Employees under this style of leadership report that they feel valued and heard. Maternalistic (or Paternalistic) leaders show concern for their people and often take an interest in employees' personal lives, making people feel more connected. In return, the leader receives trust and loyalty. The lack of competition can create a solid and committed workforce. These followers are likely to stay with the company a long time.

A potential disadvantage of this leadership style, however, is that followers can become too dependent on the leader. In today's workforce, participation and involvement is much more popular than in previous times. The Maternalistic/Paternalistic leadership style is now often seen as outdated, particularly as it can easily slip into becoming dictatorial. Despite that, it may be a useful style to employ occasionally in some circumstances and with some people who need more guidance and support. This leader takes responsibility and truly leads rather than leading by consensus.

Followers may appreciate the authentic interest that the leader has in their wellbeing and perceive that the leader understands their holistic needs, not just the needs of the team or the organisation.

THE IVORY TRADE

The ivory trade continues to put elephants in danger. Thousands are killed every year for their tusks, which are illegally bought and sold by criminals around the world. To try and protect elephants, a ban on buying and selling ivory was introduced in 1989. Since then, the illegal trade in ivory has slowed but not stopped. Poachers are still killing elephants for their ivory.

African national parks and conservation areas employ rangers to patrol on foot and in vehicles to keep poachers away. Countries work together to stop the smuggling of ivory across borders but criminal gangs have become more sophisticated in their smuggling techniques. The continued ivory trade combines with habitat loss and fragmentation to threaten elephant populations in their range. At this rate we may soon have to face a world without wild elephants.

African Buffalo are herd-living vegetarians. In this species the females vote for their travel preferences by standing up and staring in their direction of choice, and then lying down again.

The maternalistic leader. African Elephants are led by a matriarch, often the oldest female in the herd. This leader looks after her herd like a wise mother or grandmother. Age and experience are highly valued commodities in this challenging environment.

In African Elephants the alpha position commonly goes to the matriarch's oldest daughter after her death. Older females are a critical resource in this drought-sensitive environment as their knowledge assists the survival of the herd.

The political leader. Male Chimpanzees use violence, intelligence and political alliances to gain and retain power. They use all the tricks of politics. Dominant males rule in coalition, with one male holding the alpha position.

Kiss and make up. Chimpanzees are very quarrelsome but equally skilled at reconciliation. After a fight, males make up with a hug and a big smacker on the lips. We too are likely to have an evolutionary programmed desire to resolve conflict quickly.

Political alliances. In chimp society, spending time sitting together, grooming one another, is how relationships are formed and maintained. A positive relationship with powerful individuals in the troop is a way of advancing one's own rank.

Chimpanzees exhibit both our best and worst leadership traits. Benevolent Chimpanzee leaders are able to hold on to the top job much longer than unkind ones. A good political leader knows how to keep his allies sweet and takes care of those in his charge.

The egalitarian leader. Bonobo society is matriarchal as well as relatively peaceful. There are a number of older females that call the shots but males are not excluded. One of the oldest females is the alpha but they show no overt dominance.

In Bonobo troops there are equal numbers of males and females. In Chimpanzee communities only half the males survive as the stress and violence takes its toll. Bonobos, perhaps, have what all males desire: little conflict and lots of sex.

Make love, not war. Bonobos engage in sexual activity as a greeting, to resolve conflict, to reduce tension and to develop bonds. Disagreements rarely accelerate to serious hostility. This species has sex for fun and bonding, not just for conception.

Our wild cousins. Of our two equally close relatives, Bonobos represent a less violent and more egalitarian ape. We humans share an ape blueprint with behaviours that range from despotic to fair and compassionate.

What lessons can we learn from wild animals and take into the boardroom? The positive leadership examples from our wild animal cousins can help humans to lead better, more naturally, whilst meeting the expectations of their followers.

CHAPTER 9

THE POLITICAL LEADER
– CHIMPANZEE

'Chimps are very quick to have a sudden fight or aggressive episode, but they're equally as good at reconciliation.'

JANE GOODALL

Zoo visitors watching Chimpanzees might be forgiven for thinking that the biggest, meanest chimp is in charge. Well, maybe, but not for long. There are many subtleties to leadership in chimp society, just as there are in human groups. Together with the Bonobo, Chimpanzees belong to the genus *Pan* and are our closest living relatives. Fossils and genetic evidence conclude that the African apes diverged from a single common ancestor and that *Homo sapiens* diverged from Chimpanzees and Bonobos some five to seven million years ago – a relatively short time in evolutionary terms. As a result, we share just under 99 per cent of our DNA with chimps. But, strangely, we are not in the same genus. It has been postulated that if extra-terrestrial taxonomists were to land on our planet to do some classification, they would probably put us humans in the same genus as Chimpanzees and Bonobos.

To put this kinship into context, the Red-eyed Vireo and the White-eyed Vireo, two species of small American songbird, share only 97.1 per cent of their DNA but they are in the same genus, *Vireo*. All but the most keen-eyed observers would have difficulty telling these birds apart. In his book *The Rise and Fall of the Third Chimpanzee*, Jared Diamond proposes that both the Bonobo and the Chimpanzee belong with humans in the genus *Homo*, rather than in the genus *Pan*, where they are currently classified. He argues that other species have been reclassified by genus for less genetic similarity than exists between humans and chimps.

Spending time with chimps day-in, day-out as a zookeeper, it is mesmerising to see how alike they are to us – especially in their sophisticated manner of communication. Individual chimps are easy to recognise, just as we recognise the people we are familiar with. I can recognise the animals I know from the way they walk, their body posture, their daily habits, such as where they sit or how they eat, and of course, their faces. Facial expressions are a powerful communication tool for both humans and Chimpanzees. Our facial musculature is almost identical to that of Chimpanzees. The way we grin or pout or show fear matches what we see on the face of a chimp in the same situation. Chimps use facial expressions, vocalisations, body language and grooming to communicate. They smack kisses on each other's mouths to make up after a quarrel.

They pat each other on the back, they hug and greet each other after an absence. Spending time watching our primate cousins is a poignant reminder of just how similar we are.

POLITICAL LEADERSHIP – CHIMPANZEE STYLE

After humans, Chimpanzees are possibly the most politically aware species on the planet – they use all the tricks of politics to gain and retain power. Chimps are *very clear* about their desire for power and the privileges it brings, and the way they use alliances for this purpose would give Machiavelli something to think about. Humans tend to hide their desire for power and talk about 'wanting to contribute to society' instead. Our culture generally has a taboo on articulating the aspiration for power and status, but it doesn't stop many people from wanting it.

Chimpanzee groups are ruled by dominant males with one male holding the alpha position. The top position is a tenuous place in their community and stressful at the best of times with many challenges and a lot of responsibility.

Male Chimpanzees use three strategies to gain and keep power:
1. Brute strength and intimidation
2. Intelligence
3. Political alliances

In some cases a strong, large male may rise to the top position through violence and intimidation only.

Nearly all males will display their dominance at some stage, showing off their strength to the group, and sometimes these impressive bluff displays can be enough to change the leadership. Combining a good display with intelligence, however, can have an even better outcome. Jane Goodall observed a male called Mike, a fairly low-ranking individual, using his intelligence to enhance his position. At that time a large male called Goliath was the alpha male of the group in Gombe Stream National Park, Tanzania. Mike, much smaller than Goliath, found some empty kerosene cans in the researchers' camp. He carried two of these cans close to where the other chimps were sitting. He started his display as males usually do by rocking back and forth more and more vigorously, hair-on-end, hooting and incorporating the banging of kerosene cans together in his performance. Mike suddenly charged to where the other males were sitting, hitting the cans forcefully as he ran towards them. The other males fled, obviously intimidated by this display of power. The top-ranking male, Goliath, was sitting a little removed from the group and Mike, possibly encouraged by his success with the other males, decided to take on Goliath as well. He ran towards him, hooting and banging cans so convincingly that Goliath too fled into the forest. Mike was able to take over leadership (for a while) by combining his dominance display with his smartness, knowing that the noise of the cans would impress his rivals.

Chimpanzees show deference to higher ranking members of the troop with submissive greetings. After his display, Mike's new rank was confirmed by members of the group paying their respect with soft pant-grunts, crouching low as they approached. Mike's dynamic and innovative display convinced the group members of his superiority. They then surrounded Mike to groom him and be close to him. Only Goliath refused to pay his respects.

The third political strategy male Chimpanzees use is building alliances. For a male chimp to gain power or retain it he has to carefully manage his relationships with other powerful males. We know that the alpha male chimp does not only get to the top job because he's stronger than all the others. He is more likely to get the top job if he is also smart and knows how to form partnerships. If he can put together a large and steady alliance he will be able to lead the community. Coalitions have to be maintained, though. Supporters in the coalition spend nearly all their time together – they groom, share food, exchange favours and back one another during fights. Comparable coalitions probably ruled the social lives of early humans and still do today. We share with the chimps our ability to form strong bonds, establish hierarchies and hunt or fight together against perceived enemies. A chimp that is able to use a combination of dominance strategies is more likely to gain a position of leadership, or at least a position of influence.

HOW CHIMPANZEE SOCIETY WORKS

Not all human males want to be leaders, but many do. Not all male Chimpanzees try to be the leader, but many do. Higher rank for a male chimp means more privileges, in particular access to sexually receptive females and food. As with so many things in animal and human life, dominance is often about power and sex! Male Chimpanzee competition for leadership is fierce and how they manage it can be reminiscent of the alliances of politicians in the same political party. Chimps are well aware that they need each other to make their community work. They need to cooperate to fend off neighbouring troops of Chimpanzees and, like politicians, they can put their internal rivalry aside to band together against a common enemy. They achieve dominance through posturing and fighting but they have to be careful not to injure their in-group rivals too badly. Their in-clan enemy may be needed to fight on their side, as an ally, in the near future.

Chimpanzee society is about partnerships, doing favours, and keeping score of them. Chimps that are in alliance with each other expect that the giving and receiving of favours is somewhat balanced. Some of this is expressed with gestures. One of the more common hand gestures seen in Chimpanzees is 'holding out a hand'. This can mean several things depending on the circumstances. It may mean: *give me some of that food, help me in this fight*, or simply *do you want to groom?* The invitation to help during a fight is very telling and says something about existing coalitions. The requester is expecting payback for a favour. We often show similar conduct in meetings, for example, when a suggested course of action hasn't received a positive response and we call on the opinion of a sympathiser in the hope they offer support. Particularly if we have supported this person previously in a similar situation. Support from an ally during a meeting can make all the difference – once two or three group members are over the line the group may be moved to agreement.

Young males start to advertise their leadership aspirations in their teenage years by displaying frequently. In Taronga Zoo metal doors are used to separate the outdoor and indoor Chimpanzee spaces. Like Mike in Jane Goodall's study, the male chimps frequently use these doors as percussive props to enhance their dominance displays. They take a fast run up towards the doors and at the last moment, turning in the air, they give the door an almighty thump with both feet. This makes a reverberating loud noise which the chimps must find very satisfying. Males in the Taronga colony employ different techniques to individualise their dominance display, almost like a signature.

Chimps are enormously strong. Although smaller than humans – males weigh up to 60kg (130lb) – Chimpanzees have been shown to be about as strong as several adult male humans comparable in size. When they confront members from their own troop they use a form of controlled fighting and they rarely injure their in-clan rivals severely. Injuries inflicted by females upon in-clan members are usually restricted to bites on hands and feet. Males in more serious fights may cause wounds to the head, neck or genitals of their opponent. Clashes with members from other chimp communities are not so controlled and wounding can be quite severe, even leading to death. When it comes to struggles for leadership, one way or another, chimps and humans both have to find a balance between competition and maintaining order, especially with a view to keeping their alliances on board.

Conflict in Chimpanzee troops is frequent, but so is reconciliation. Even if one chimp has wounded another it is common to see them sitting together, grooming some hours later. Reconciliation is seen after almost every fight. Sometimes this is within minutes, at other times it may take a few hours. Making up after a fight involves kissing – an open-mouthed smack on the lips – embracing and then grooming. Bonobos also reconcile after skirmishes but rather than kissing and hugging they go all the way and reconcile with sex. This happens regardless of the gender of the Bonobos involved – male and male, male and female and female and female – and either copulation or mutual genital contact is used. This shows a strong inclination in both Bonobos and Chimpanzees to resolve conflicts. We have the same need for resolving conflict with those in our community. Not doing so can make us feel anxious and uncomfortable until the disagreement is resolved. This probably means that we too have evolved to resolve conflict quickly because as a social species we may suffer emotionally if we don't reconcile quickly. We may not thrive as a group or as individuals if we nurse grievances and are at odds within our clan.

Greeting amongst Chimpanzees is a sort of confirmation of one's ranking in the hierarchy. Some bowing and scraping has to be done by low-ranking males to those of higher rank. At the same time the dominant male will try and look bigger by stretching himself to seem taller and by making his hair stand on end. This is not dissimilar to the kind of conduct I have seen in business meetings. Subordinate Chimpanzee males will greet their superiors with an action called 'bobbing'. This looks remarkably like the bowing we see in some cultures, like Japan or when we meet royalty. When I see someone bowing to the Queen, I often think of the hierarchal greetings of chimps. It gives an entirely different perspective on our social and cultural customs.

In addition to bowing, females will usually present their bottoms for inspection to the dominant ape. Chimpanzees can be dangerous and as a young keeper I was told what to do if I ever unexpectedly found myself in the presence of an angry chimp. The best thing, the male keepers told me, would be to drop your trousers and present your bottom as an act of submission. Luckily, I've never had to take this drastic action and I am not sure that I would or could recommend it to anyone else either!

READY FOR LEADERSHIP OR NOT!

Sometimes we can find ourselves in a situation that makes us a leader whether we want to be one or not. It can take some time for a person to get used to being a leader, rather than being one of the troop. The following story is about how Taronga chimp Lubutu found himself thrust into the alpha role after the untimely death of his predecessor – a situation we humans can find ourselves in too, such as when a promotion happens before we are ready for it.

Allan Schmidt, a veteran great ape keeper at Taronga Zoo, has known Lubutu for most of his life. He was there when Lubutu first found himself getting promoted to the top job:

'As he was still a youngster he was not ready for leadership and unable to physically dominate the females. He was only eight years old at the time but, due to circumstances, was the oldest male in the group. Males in human care with good and reliable nutrition usually reach their adult size at about ten or eleven years of age, and few years later in the wild. It was interesting to see that the females (all bar one) did submit to him, evidenced by paying respect, by 'bowing' to him and soliciting his help during spats with others. The females must have realised there was a need to have an alpha male and accepted him in that role. Lubutu himself was not comfortable in his new-found seniority. He was extremely reluctant to resolve conflict as his job demanded, realising perhaps that he did not have the strength to follow through with discipline, if that were needed.

When the females were squabbling, Lubutu seemed to think that pretending it was not happening was his best strategy. He essentially ignored conflict in the group between the ages of eight and ten. Once he did reach his maximum body size, his 'fence sitting' was no longer tolerated by the females. They expected more from their leader. It took him a while to appreciate that he had a role to play. Little by little, he learned to be the leader he is now.'

Lubutu has been the alpha male in the Taronga group for some sixteen years now. The females like him because is a relatively gentle leader. One way he keeps the peace among the males is by not being too exclusive in his control of sexually receptive females. That's how Lubutu keeps his loyal lieutenants sweet – something many Chimpanzee males would not tolerate.

'Taronga's previous alpha male, Snowy, would be livid if he caught sight of another male coupling with a female. He'd run the length of the enclosure to break them up. Lubutu is not too bothered if he sees the other males mate with one of his females. This tolerance towards the sexual exploits of the other males in the group probably helps to keep Lubutu in power. As long as everyone gets what they desire, the urge to overthrow the leader is less strong. Lubutu maintains the support he needs by keeping the balance between the messages: *I am big, tough and dominant* and *I am also a nice guy*. He displays his dominance with impressive bluff performances, grooms males he needs to keep close, shares food, and is very respectful of mothers with infants.'

Power is a natural aspect of life for a hierarchal society. New leaders need to find their feet to know how much control to exert for the job to be done. The challenge is to use power fairly and for the greater good of the community. An alpha chimp using his intelligence in leadership maintains just enough power to keep control. Too much power makes too many enemies.

CHIMPANZEES DON'T MAKE GOOD PETS

Chimpanzee babies are irresistibly cute and it might seem that raising one would fun. Chimps are popular as pets in many areas of the world, despite their strength. A baby chimp spends all its time clinging to its mother, needing her love and care around the clock. As they grow, so does their strength. Some Chimpanzee pet owners have been severely injured, losing fingers and sustaining serious facial injuries. I once had to entertain a young Chimpanzee whilst his mother was undergoing a health check. The youngster was about two years old and it took two of us to keep him under some semblance of control.

As they grow up, chimps often become destructive and resent any form of discipline. Despite initial good intentions, most Chimpanzee owners decide to give the animal up when it becomes impossible to handle. Zoos will likely not accept a Chimpanzee that does not understand how to behave in chimp society because it will cause too much disruption in the established group. Tragically, many ex-pet chimps end up in medical research laboratories, spending the rest of lives subjected to testing regimes. Chimpanzees in human care may reach fifty or sixty years of age. In most countries and states there are laws prohibiting the private ownership of Chimpanzees.

GIRL POWER IN CHIMPANZEE SOCIETY

Female chimps, although subordinate to males, have significant influence in their societies. Allan Schmidt tells an intriguing story about the role of females in a leadership challenge.

'Alpha male Lubutu had been removed from the group temporarily to have a vasectomy. The next day he was still recovering from the anaesthetic. As Lubutu rejoined the group in the outdoor chimp habitat Shabani, a male one year younger than him who had been biding his time, saw his opportunity with Lubutu's control being at a low ebb. Shabani is a much more aggressive individual and uses his strength to intimidate. He humiliated Lubutu by chasing him up the highest climbing structure and keeping him there by charging repeatedly. I remember seeing Lubutu at the top fear grinning and asking anybody for help, while Shabani stalked around the bottom, keeping him running scared. I was thinking that this would be the day that Shabani took over the leadership. When the chimps were brought into the night-house that evening Lubutu was completely surrounded by females, grooming him and forming a protective cordon around him. Meanwhile, Shabani was sitting by himself in the corner. I think that's when Shabani got his epiphany moment. The females simply did not support him. They probably did not want a leader who was overly aggressive. So from then on we saw Shabani change his ways. Before this event he would never tolerate the youngsters nearby and he rarely shared food with females – all things that Lubutu does very well. After this event, Shabani played with the kids, groomed females and shared food with them. The females at Taronga see Lubutu as pretty much a nice guy. He can discipline when he needs to but basically he's very easy going. Having the choice between Lubutu and an overly aggressive Shabani, the females naturally thought: 'Well, we're not having that.' This leadership challenge happened some nine years ago and Lubutu continues to be the leader of the group. Shabani is now the lowest ranked male of the five adult males in the troop.'

There is a lot to say about the males, their threat or bluff displays, their alliances and conflict resolutions. Female Chimpanzees however also have a crucial role in the community. Research of wild Chimpanzees shows that it is common to find an alpha male kept in line by female consensus. Although adult females are almost always submissive to adult males, they too have their ranking in the hierarchy, influenced by who they are related to and their reproductive status. Conflict between females is much more sporadic than conflict between males. It has been suggested that female status amongst females seems to be based on respect rather than intimidation. The influence of an older female in the troop in particular must not be underestimated. Frans de Waal, in his book *Chimpanzee Politics,* first described how female chimps at Arnhem Zoo in the Netherlands repeatedly walked up to a displaying male to remove a stone from his hand before he could use it to injure a rival. De Waal saw this behaviour sometimes several times a day.

Older females play an important role in peacemaking. I too have regularly seen females in the Taronga Zoo colony mediate between fighting males. They go out of their way trying to make males reconcile. A female will sit close to one of the males after a spat and groom him for a while, presumably to calm him down. She will then slowly make her way to where the other male is sitting, checking and looking back to see if the male she was grooming is following her. If he's not, she may go back and grab him by the arm to make him follow her. When the female then sits close to the second male, both males will groom her until she walks off a little later. The two males then have to deal with each other. They groom one another and in the process reconcile their differences.

Females will also protest loudly when a dominant male continues to chase another in order to beat him up. Some years ago, I saw Gombe, a previous dominant male in the Taronga zoo colony, regularly chase other males with whom he had a score to settle.

Before Gombe could catch his chosen victim, however, the females would vocalise loudly – a bark-like sound – to protest against Gombe's aggression. Gombe, grinning nervously, would more often than not give up on the attack.

A female's power is at its strongest when she's at her most attractive to the males; when she's in season. Important high-ranking males will seek her company. When a female Chimpanzee comes into oestrus, her most sexually receptive time, her genital area swells. Those swellings vary in size – some females have swellings as big as a football and others have much smaller protuberances – and they rise and fall over ten days, shrinking back to normal size eventually. This swelling happens at the midpoint between menstrual periods when the females are courted insistently by the males. Jane Goodall comments on this feature by stating: 'Many times, as I have watched a huge swollen female Chimpanzee adjusting her position time and time again, trying to get comfortable on some branch or hard rock, I have thanked evolution for sparing human females a similar periodic disfigurement, though designers and manufacturers of bustles would, I suppose, have been in clover.' I, too, have always thought how lucky we are, given how much genetic similarity we have with Chimpanzees, that this is one feature we do not have in common.

Females are an important emotional support for their offspring. Young chimps being told off by an adult will run to their mother for support. Even alpha males remain 'mama's-boys' their entire lives. Often, when they are upset after an altercation with another male, they will run to their mother for a hug.

WHAT CAN WE LEARN FROM CHIMPANZEE POLITICAL LEADERSHIP?

Simon Duffy, Chair of the Jane Goodall Institute, and Director of Wildlife Conservation and Science at Taronga Zoo, shares his thoughts on leadership from working closely with Chimpanzees:

'I spent some time observing chimps in a sanctuary in the Democratic Republic of Congo. When I first arrived there were two big mature males, they were huge and were displaying their dominance in spades. I thought for sure that one of these was the alpha male. As I spent more time watching, it appeared that a younger, smaller, chimp was the leader of the group.

After watching them all for a while longer, I understood why. Whilst the two bigger males were bluff displaying their dominance to impress or intimidate, the younger chimp would be further to the back working on his relationships with the others in the troop. He was calm but confident and seemed to invest a lot of his time in looking after and supporting the other chimps. His name was Congo. All Chimpanzees in this sanctuary are orphans and therefore unrelated. In the wild, Chimpanzees rely on family coalitions for support. Congo really invested in his relationships within the group, not favouring one chimp over another. He seemed to know what approach he needed for each member. When it was the big dominant males, he would show respect but be confident with them. With the older females he would sit and groom them. He would even play with babies. Congo is still the leader now, some eleven years after I first met him.

I learned from Congo that to be a good leader it helps to be calm and confident. Your group looks to you to be a tranquil influence. That calmness filters out to the group. If you, as the leader, lose your cool or become frenzied then everyone else does too. There are times in my roles that I've been thinking: 'Oh no, what am I going to do here?' But I have learned from Congo to stay relaxed. I've got to be calm, if I want everyone else to be calm.'

While there are despotic Chimpanzee leaders, there are also very good ones like Congo and Lubutu. An alpha who rules by terror inevitably loses the support of all the other males, who then end up uniting against him, deposing him, often in a violent way. Despite their better qualities, Chimpanzees are masters at the divide-and-rule tactics we often see in our own societies. They excel at building male alliances whilst ensuring that the other males don't get close enough to each other to potentially organise a coup. Jane Goodall noted that the average reign of chimps who relied primarily on intimidation was only about two years, while those who focused more on coalition-building and smartness ended up staying at the top for ten years or more. An alpha male needs to know when to use force and also when to be nice. Allan Schmidt has an apt saying about chimp leadership: 'It is a balancing act; hitting someone over the head with one hand and doling out food with the other.'

Political chimps, like political leaders in our society, have negative and positive traits. It is up to us, which of these we want to emulate. I emphasise the positive traits of this political leader though because there are many positive traits. Being a good Chimpanzee leader is hard work. There are many demands on this individual and he has to really nurture his relationships to keep the top job. Chimp troops are reciprocal societies – favours are exchanged and a good alpha male is the hub of this, making sure he includes everyone.

Chimp leadership is about maintaining troop cohesion and harmony. This is done by settling disputes fast, consoling the distressed, and ensuring the fair distribution of resources. The alpha male himself is more likely to think that his top priority is impregnating as many females as possible. However, as with most jobs, multi-tasking is necessary.

WHAT DO CHIMPANZEE FOLLOWERS EXPECT FROM THEIR POLITICAL LEADER?

The constant threat of being usurped by another ambitious male is balanced against the privileges of the alpha position: sex and power. Because it is only his alliances that keep him in the alpha position it is of real interest to look at what the followers get out of this deal. Followers want a leader who is fair, tolerant and shares resources. They also expect the alpha, with the help of his loyal followers, to defend the group from intruders and settle disputes. Male followers are more likely to support a leader who does not monopolise sex with the females. Leaders who do this are usually overthrown by a coalition of males who may have supported him previously.

Female chimps benefit from an alpha male who is not given to violent rages on a too-frequent basis, who spends time with them grooming, plays with or is at least tolerant of the youngsters in the group, shares food, and keeps the violence of other males under control. Followers benefit from a leader who uses enough power to keep the peace without unnecessary violence.

WHEN WOULD WE USE CHIMPANZEE POLITICAL LEADERSHIP?

The Chimpanzee leader has a lot of demands to balance and it is not unusual for alpha males to suffer stress. Heart attacks can occur in high-ranking male Chimpanzees just as they do in overly stressed corporate leaders. Looking at global leadership today, it is remarkable how much of what happens in the world mimics the goings-on in a Chimpanzee troop – ambition, bluff dominance displays, the potential for violence, an obsession with sex, the cultivation of valuable connections – to name a few.

Just as no two Chimpanzees are the same, so Chimpanzee leaders vary. Some are better than others in serving their community's needs and keeping as much stability as is possible in a chimp troop. What they all have in common, though, is that they can't maintain the alpha position without a coalition of support – support of other high-ranking males in particular, but also the support of females. The influence of older males and females on how that coalition works should not be underestimated. Those older individuals should be seen as the elder statesmen and women of chimp communities. Their influence behind the throne can make or break leaders. In our workplaces, the positive alliances we form with co-workers are as important as they are in chimp troops. They make us work as a team, support each other and probably make us happier.

The political leadership style is common in our society although we don't always call it that. People are also driven by hierarchy and some, but not all, by power. Understanding these drivers helps us to understand the workplace. We can take the good, more altruistic aspects of this leadership style as an example of our better nature. We share a common ancestor with both Chimpanzees and Bonobos. Bonobos, as we will see in the next chapter, have a very different, more egalitarian, approach to leadership than Chimpanzees. As Frans de Waal states: 'The fundamental difference between our two closest relatives is that one resolves sexual issues with power, while the other resolves power issues with sex.'

Good Chimpanzee leadership is not only about being in charge. It is about taking care of those in their charge. A good Chimpanzee leader has privileges but works *for* the members of their troop. Not the other way around.

A DEATH IN THE FAMILY

Fifi was the grand old dame of our chimp society. At sixty she had reached a veritable age, surpassing the average life expectancy of forty-five years for the species. She had more and more trouble getting about, and climbing had not been an option for some time. She looked old, with her grey-haired face and greying flanks. She had earned the right to take it easy and enjoy the care and attention lavished on her by her dedicated keepers in her twilight years. She had been ailing for a few days and had been spoiled with extra treats. Rather than joining the troop outside, Fifi prepared her nest in the night-house. She died peacefully during the day in July 2007. Normally the troop vocalises loudly as they come into the night-house, expressing their excitement at coming inside and finding food. This time they filed past and stared at Fifi's lifeless body, silent and subdued. All the chimps in the troop paid their respects to the old lady. Fifi's family sat quietly with her and her sixteen-year-old daughter, Kuma, touched her hand. The whole group stayed subdued for days as they grieved for their grand old dame.

CHAPTER 10

THE EGALITARIAN LEADER — BONOBO

'If you watch animals objectively for any length of time, you're driven to the conclusion that their main aim in life is to pass on their genes to the next generation.'

DAVID ATTENBOROUGH

Bonobo. The word alone conjures up something exotic and exciting. Bonobos have a reputation among the great ape researchers as the *make-love-not-war-ape* or the *hippie-ape*. The French call Bonobos the *Left Bank Chimpanzee*, the left bank of the Seine in Paris being famous, historically, for its artists and Bohemian inhabitants. Bonobos live south of the Congo River, whereas Chimpanzees live on the northern side.

Bonobos may at first glance look like a small Chimpanzee. A

second look will show a longer-limbed ape with a mop of black hair parted on top of the head, making the ears stand out less. Pink-lipped and dark-faced, Bonobos are a handsome, graceful primate, perhaps more elegant-looking than Chimpanzees. When it comes to behaviour, however, the two species differ in more important ways. Bonobo society is often described as peaceful and egalitarian compared with that of the more hierarchal Chimpanzee.

Vanessa Woods, in her delightful book *Bonobo Handshake*, describes her observations of the difference between Chimpanzees and Bonobos in relation to food sharing tests conducted in Lola Ya Bonobo Sanctuary in the Congo:

'Chimpanzees eat like Americans. They can down a pile of bananas in a New York minute. There is no eye contact. Very little conversation. It's more refuelling a car than sharing a meal, and afterward the dining area looks like a bomb went off. Bonobos eat like the French. No one is happy unless lunch takes three hours. There is a lot of talking in between courses ('Will you have a bite of pineapple with your mango?' 'Oh no, please, you first…'). Peels are folded back delicately; seeds are carefully removed. The meal is all about company, and afterward, everyone lounges about in a food coma, grooming and staring at the sky.'

EGALITARIAN LEADERSHIP – BONOBO STYLE

Egalitarianism comes from the French '*égal*' *meaning equal*. But what makes Bonobos more egalitarian than many other species? Firstly, females dominate the Bonobo troops, but there is no exclusion of the males. The lower ranking animals can be of either gender. All members of the troop get enough to eat and sharing food is common. Bonobos will also have sex with any member of their group and respect for hierarchy is not overtly enforced. In Chimpanzee society there is much more display of rank as subordinates must grovel and bow to appease superior animals. Researchers studying Bonobos find it much harder to establish who is the alpha is as there is not as much reason to display dominance in a more peaceful community.

In nature, primary bonding is usually with same-sex kin in the natal group, that is the group into which an animal is born. We see this in male Chimpanzees, female Savanna Baboons, the Spotted Hyena and elephants. Bonobo females, however, are an exception to this general rule, having strong bonds with their sons, with whom they form alliances. The real evidence of this exception, however, can be seen in Bonobo female coalitions. Young female Bonobos migrate into another troop at puberty and then form strong bonds with same-sex strangers over time. This secondary bonding with non-kin sets up powerful artificial sisterhoods capable of running the show.

One way to consider why this unusual matriarchal and egalitarian social system has developed is because it keeps the young safe. Male Chimpanzees occasionally kill infants in their group, as do humans, unfortunately. Nahoko Tokuyama and Takeshi Furuichi postulate that coalitions in female Bonobos might have evolved as a counterstrategy to male harassment. They also found that females defeated males more easily when they formed coalitions than when they confronted males alone. Tokuyama and Furuichi also suggest that these coalitions might in fact increase gregariousness among females, allowing females to develop friendly interactions that promote tolerance. Female Bonobos spend time together grooming, eating and socialising. Fighting between males and females is rare and males are generally patient around juveniles and infants. The killing of babies and infants, which happens in chimp troops, is almost non-existent in Bonobos. The older females are the crucial contributors to maintaining a more egalitarian and cohesive society.

HOW BONOBOS LIVE – MATRIARCHAL SOCIETY

Bonobos are matriarchal, with females calling the shots and social relations being female-led and dominated. They live, however, in mixed-gender communities usually made up of thirty to eighty individuals, where males are readily integrated, despite female bonds being stronger. In most animal societies where a dominance hierarchy exists, the dominant gender is likely to be male and physically larger and stronger. Bonobos are unusual in that the females are smaller than the males by an average 15 per cent in body weight and lack the sharp canine teeth of the males. Yet in Bonobo communities females rule!

Unlike chimps, female Bonobo camaraderie triumphs and the bonds between the males are feeble. 'It's a matriarchy' states Amy Parish, a primatologist from the University of California. 'Females are running the show.' While female chimps must mate with all males, the leader of Bonobo community ensures that the females can refuse a male's sexual advances without fearing subsequent violence.

Bonobo societies are relatively peaceful compared with those of Chimpanzees. Disagreements rarely accelerate to serious hostility. On the whole, Bonobos are far less violent than their Chimpanzee cousins. Whereas the male Chimpanzee uses aggression to advance his rank, Bonobos males do not compete for dominance. The lower ranks of Bonobo communities are balanced in gender, with some males outranking some females and vice versa. But the highest-ranking individuals in the group are always old females. Male Bonobos do not build alliances with other males and there is no evidence of mortal wounding between them.

THE EGALITARIAN LEADER – OLD GIRLS RULE!

Much less is known about Bonobos than about Chimpanzees. However, most of the research in the wild and in zoos confirms that the highest-ranking individuals in a Bonobo troop are always the old girls. Although there tends to be a number of old females at high rank, it is generally believed that one of the oldest is the alpha. What makes the hierarchy system even more intriguing is that Bonobo are patrilineal, with troops being made up of generation after generation of related males who stay in the group their entire lives, while adolescent females will migrate to join another troop, thereby ensuring genetic variety. The lads only derive their status from their immigrant mother. The bond between mothers and their sons is strong and these bonds continue throughout life. While rank does not play as important a role in Bonobo society as it does in other primate groups, it does still feature. For example, the son of a very high-ranking female will also derive a higher social status, which may outrank another female. However, the son always depends on his mother for support. Even as a fully-grown adult, he will still follow his old mother and ask for her help. Once she dies, the son's social status goes down, because he has no female supporter left.

The type of leadership that best describes Bonobos is egalitarian. An example of this egalitarian leadership is given by Gottfried Hohmann, a Bonobo specialist at the Max Planck Institute for Evolutionary Anthropology in Leipzig, Germany. Hohmann describes what happens when a Bonobo kills a monkey or a forest antelope:

'If the hunter reveals his or her prize to the rest of the group, an old female will eventually come and place her arm over it, calmly taking possession. Then, other Bonobos will gather around, arms outstretched for their share. The old females are not monopolising the food. They allow others to participate, but in a controlled way.'

As in many social animal communities, the way decisions about 'where we go next and when' are made is a good indicator of how the community is organised and who is in charge. Nahoko Tokuyama and Takeshi Furuichi conducted extensive research of Bonobos at Wamba in the Democratic Republic of Congo and found that the individuals who were more central to the grooming core initiated departures more frequently. They confirmed that old females kick off departures more often. The old girls are likely to be followed because of the support they give to the younger females. They also have more knowledge about food availability in their roaming territory.

THE BONOBO AS BUSHMEAT

In Africa, the forest is called 'the bush', and anything hunted in the forest and eaten is 'bushmeat'. For indigenous Africans, bushmeat is traditional fare. When there was a small human population and a large healthy wildlife population this was not the problem that it is today. However, as human populations grow exponentially and forests disappear rapidly, the eating of bushmeat is putting a lot of wild animals under additional pressure.

The greatest threat to Bonobos is poaching for the commercial bushmeat trade. There is a massive demand for bushmeat stemming from the cities within the Democratic Republic of Congo. Rebel factions and poorly-paid government soldiers aid the flow of guns and facilitate the supply of bushmeat. In some areas there are local taboos against eating Bonobo meat but these traditions are changing fast as cultural values shift. Among the Bongando people, an ethnic group living in and around the village of Wamba, where much of the research on the Bonobo has taken place, it has traditionally been taboo to eat Bonobo. In Bongando folklore, Bonobos are classified not as animals, but as human beings, due to the resemblance of Bonobos and their behaviour towards humans. The International Union for the Conservation of Nature lists the Bonobo as Endangered. It urgently recommends stricter enforcement of wildlife laws and more effective management throughout the Bonobo's range.

FEMALE COALITIONS

Bonobo society works because older females support younger females against male misdemeanours. Bonobos, like the Spotted Hyena and some other matriarchal animal species, established the *#MeToo* movement well before we did. If the females stand united, the males remain policed and therefore stay respectful. Females can form strong bonds when an older female steps in to defend a younger member of the community who is in an accelerating clash with a resident male. The older female's social standing and the fact there are now two in battle with the male usually guarantees that the females get the upper hand in the argument.

Although much less violent than Chimpanzees, when females attack it can become quite vicious, dispelling somewhat the 'entirely peace-loving' image that is often portrayed about Bonobos. All observers can usually see is a furry ball of arms and legs with much accompanying high-pitched screaming. Invariably it is the male who sustains injuries. These incidents are not common and would indicate that the male has seriously breached the moral code.

Adult females react to a wide variety of male aggravations. A male may have overstepped the mark with unwanted sexual advances, by monopolising food or by just being a nuisance. Any male who harms an infant can expect severe punishment. The aggression that descends upon such an offender suggests that a strong moral code protects a troop's most defenceless members. Those in charge will retort by forming a posse of two or more females and jointly take on the bully. By working together, members of the somewhat smaller gender are able to protect themselves against unwanted behaviour and by doing so they force the males to behave respectfully.

SEX IN BONOBO SOCIETY

How does the hypersexuality of Bonobos fit with the kind of organisation in which they live? In most mammal groups, females are sexually receptive for a couple of days around ovulation. Bonobos, however, are known to engage in sexual activity as a greeting, to resolve conflict, to reduce tension and to form bonds. Before Frans de Waal studied Bonobos in San Diego Zoo in 1983, we thought ourselves to be the only species on the planet to have sex for fun and bonding, and not just for conception. De Waal reported Bonobos performing tongue kissing, fellatio and a whole *Kama Sutra* of sexual positions. Sexual encounters in Bonobos are exhibited in all combinations of ages and genders. The only taboo appears to be between mothers and their sons. As young Bonobo females leave their natal group as teenagers there is no chance of them mating with their father or brothers.

Frans de Waal, in his book *Our Inner Ape; Best and Worst of Human Nature*, describes two females in San Diego Zoo, Loretta, and a newly arrived female Bonobo embrace and rub each other's genitals upon meeting. He states: 'They had big grins on their faces and squealed loudly, leaving little doubt about whether apes know sexual pleasure.' Until that time, Loretta was subordinate to a male called Vernon who ruled the group because it was small and Loretta was the only female. Once Loretta had a female companion the writing was on the wall for Vernon's position of power. Within months he was asking for food from the females with an outstretched hand. Vernon's fall from power underscores the importance of the female coalition in Bonobos. One way they maintain their harmony is that females reconcile quickly after any squabbles, and sometimes with sex. Their female-led groups can't afford any kinks in their armour of solidarity.

COMPARING BONOBOS WITH CHIMPANZEES

Comparing and contrasting the leadership and dominance behaviour of our two equally closest relatives to that of humans is inevitable. Although we know much more about Chimpanzee behaviour than we do about that of Bonobos, it is still worth discussing. Researchers who studied the species either in zoos or in the wild often mention that Bonobos are more egalitarian than Chimpanzees. Bonobo leadership reflects that egalitarian nature in their more peaceful communities. Researchers report that it takes a long time to see clear evidence of the hierarchy in Bonobos, although there is one. In chimps it does not take too long to see who is in charge and who would like to be. The explicit submissive conduct towards the alpha as seen in chimps is very subtle in Bonobos. The older female in charge and her posse of female supporters run a tight ship in which food is shared, violence is minimal and babies are cherished and protected. Even sexual activity is egalitarian and available to all.

WHAT'S IN A NAME?

Bonobos were only 'discovered' to be different from Chimpanzees in the 1920s. The name given to them at the time was 'Pygmy Chimpanzee'. The Bonobo is not much smaller than the Chimpanzee so this is a bit of a misnomer. Could the name could possibly refer to the pygmy peoples who lived in the same area?

The name 'Bonobo' first appeared in literature in 1954, when two German scientists, Eduard Paul Tratz and Heinz Heck, suggested it as a new name for Pygmy Chimpanzees. There is a theory that the name 'Bonobo' could have originated from a misspelling on a shipping crate from Bolobo, a town on the Congo River, close to where the first Bonobos were collected from the wild in the 1920s.

WHAT CAN WE LEARN FROM THE BONOBO EGALITARIAN LEADERSHIP STYLE?

According to Hohmann: 'Bonobos prove that it is possible for a peaceful, egalitarian society to emerge. There are mechanisms in nature that do not promote the use of violence and aggression, Bonobos are a wonderful example of that.'

Hierarchy and egalitarianism are *not* mutually exclusive. All social animal groups have some form of hierarchy, and the ranking of individuals takes place in nature to avoid conflict rather than create it. Despite the fact that a hierarchy exists in Bonobo troops, they are capable of maintaining a more equal social culture. We, too, live in inherently hierarchal societies but are also able to create a good deal of equality within them. Social standing is important to humans, whether it's our position in a team, within an organisation or in our friendship groups. Just like Bonobos, alliances and bonding are important to us. Bonobo females, despite their smaller size, are able to form coalitions that make them powerful enough to control any wayward behaviour of the larger, stronger gender and thus maintain a peaceable society.

Bonobo leadership is about the fair division of food, the survival of offspring and creating a harmonious society that thrives. Equitable Bonobo leaders protect the vulnerable members of their community. The leaders are the ones to share the food around and set an egalitarian example by making sure everyone gets to eat.

WHAT DO BONOBO FOLLOWERS EXPECT FROM THEIR EGALITARIAN LEADERS?

Bonobos follow the old female leaders because they know where to find food and share the resources fairly. The young females who migrate to new groups benefit from the protection of the older females. The advantages for the followers in this type of leadership are obvious: food and sex are more or less equally distributed and there is minimal aggression. Birth ratios for male and female Chimpanzees and Bonobos are about 50:50 between boy and girl babies. In adulthood there are equal numbers of males and females in Bonobo troops but in Chimpanzee communities only half the males survive to adulthood. Chimp males would struggle to get a good life insurance policy because male mortality is extremely high in chimp troops. There are two adult females for every chimp male. The stress and violence in the Chimpanzee troops takes its toll on the adult males.

Bonobos do not appear to be as territorial as chimps and encounters with neighbouring troops tend to end in sex for all and food sharing rather than fighting. Infanticide is unheard of in Bonobos. Because of frequent non-conceptive sex, males can never be sure of the paternity of infants in the group. Killing one's own infants defeats the purpose of reproductive sex, which is to produce offspring. For the species as a whole, lack of infanticide is a major advantage to this leadership style. Admittedly, there is some nepotism with mothers advancing the interests of their sons, just as nepotism is rife in human societies. Additionally, the males are arguably 'under the thumb' but they have a significantly better quality of life than female chimps do under male leadership. Perhaps on reflection, male Bonobos have what many males desire: devolved responsibility, little conflict and lots of sex.

WHEN WOULD WE USE THE EGALITARIAN LEADERSHIP STYLE?

Egalitarian leaders in human society believe in equality for all. Egalitarianism means equal opportunity for people regardless of gender, ethnicity, sexual orientation, disability, class, or any other characteristic of difference. The egalitarian leader involves the team in decisions about new directions and builds consensus. This leadership style would work well in organisations that have a strong ethos – a well-developed sense of purpose and vision. However, consensus and planning take time and this leader has to be patient. This style may not suit a leader or a team who need immediate results. Under this leadership style staff need to be motivated, experienced and mature enough to deliver results.

The egalitarian management structure is an accepted model in business but few companies implement it fully. A combination of egalitarian and hierarchical structures is more likely to be used, just as it is in Bonobo troops. Combining a hierarchy with the principles of egalitarianism allows greater freedoms without eliminating all boundaries. Flexible boundaries mean that staff can self-direct and collaborate while overall supervision remains. This leadership style means treating people as equals, paying fairly and providing opportunities to contribute ideas and knowledge in the workplace.

Like Bonobos, egalitarian leaders do not display their status and power too openly. Egalitarian leaders maintain a perception of equality despite the fact that they do have the final say. These leaders value input from their followers but are not likely to call them that! Egalitarian leaders, like Bonobos, act with modesty and avoid frequent dominance displays. We could do much worse than emulate this leadership style in our societies as it satisfies our innate desire for fairness, compassion and a certain amount of freedom.

CHIMPANZEE AND BONOBO DNA

The latest DNA research suggests that the Bonobo and the Chimpanzee separated from each other less than one to two million years ago. Neither Bonobo nor Chimpanzee are great swimmers and the formation of the Congo River, one and half to two million years ago, possibly led to the separation of the two species. Bonobos are now found south of the Congo River whilst Chimpanzees live to the north. The *Pan* species – Chimpanzee and Bonobo – separated from our last common ancestor five or six million years ago. We seem to be the only species in the human line that has survived that separation from the common ancestor. This makes both chimps and Bonobos equally close relatives of humans.

CHAPTER 11

LEADERS AND FOLLOWERS UNITED WILL NEVER BE DEFEATED

*'Empathy is the most important instrument
in the leader's toolbox.'*

SIMON SINEK

Leaders need followers. Wild animal leaders need others to allow them to lead. This is also true in our own societies. From the democratically elected to dictators, all leaders need to surround themselves with people willing to support them. The only way they can hold their position in the longer term is if the immediate group allows this to happen. The leader has to win and keep their trust and loyalty.

Managers in our workplaces are not usually chosen by their subordinates. People good at their technical job can get promoted and suddenly find themselves responsible for the work and job satisfaction of others. Their motivation to lead may not come from a natural inclination to do so but sometimes more from an interest in the status or remuneration that promotion brings.

Animals in leadership positions often do have a real interest in leading the group. Although animals are also influenced by the perks of the job, they frequently have to fight, literally, to get or keep the alpha position. Ideally people in leadership positions should have a real interest in their subordinates and in leading people. If they don't really want to lead but only reap the immediate rewards, the followers will feel this lack of interest in them as people. Leading a group is difficult. New animal leaders have to learn the job of leading and sometimes those lessons come the hard way, just as they did for reluctant chimp leader Lubutu in Chapter 9. Being a leader is a new experience for everybody at some time in their lives and most people need time to grow in that role.

In nature, animals will often choose their leader. They may support an individual vying for the job or attach themselves to another group with a different leader. Humans do this too. The saying goes that: 'Employees join companies but leave managers'. A US Gallup poll of more than one million people found that the main reason people voluntarily left their job was a 'bad boss'. Even if the job was good, 75 per cent of people reported that if the relationship with their supervisor was not healthy they would quit.

Leaders and followers are essentially in the same boat. People and animals need good leadership and leaders need loyal followers.

There are strengths in being a follower that are often not recognised. The word 'follower' does not really do justice to the power followers have. Followers can be influencers, supporters, admirers, devotees and fans. They can form formidable coalitions or factions. In politics, factions can be extremely powerful. They can hold the balance of power in the party or bring a government to its knees. Any leader would be advised to heed the power of the followers and when unified, leaders and followers can be formidable.

POWER FROM BELOW

The influence of followers on the leadership is sometimes overlooked. Unless you are the 'leader of the world' we are all followers in some way or another. Followers have enormous power. They can elect leaders, join a union, go on strike, have a 'vote of no-confidence' or change jobs. Significant historical events celebrate the power of followers disobeying a leader.

The mutiny on the *Bounty* is a famous example of followers taking control. Lieutenant Fletcher Christian, unhappy with the reportedly despotic Captain William Bligh, led his crewmen to seize control of their ship in the Pacific in 1789. The mutineers set Captain Bligh and eighteen men loyal to him adrift in the ship's open launch. Christian and his men variously settled on Tahiti, Pitcairn Island and Norfolk Island, where their descendants can still be traced today.

People who don't appear to have any power can find that a small step towards making a stand can have considerable consequences. This was demonstrated in the case of the Gurindji stockmen who protested for equal pay for the first time in 1966, at Union Camp, Newcastle Waters Station, about 270km (170 miles) north of Tennant Creek in Australia's Northern Territory. Aboriginal stockmen, who had been the backbone of the Australian cattle industry, had never been paid wages equal to those of their white workmates. Head stockman Vincent Lingiari stepped up to lead the group's demands for better wages and working conditions. Although the workers did not win their entitlements as a result of the strike, it started a groundswell of resistance to the appalling working conditions imposed on Aboriginal people. The industrial action drew national attention, soon growing into the more fundamental concerns about their traditional lands. The strike eventually morphed into the first successful land claim under the leadership of Lingiari. From small steps, big steps can come. This first Aboriginal walk-off brought about a big cultural change in Australia.

Globally there are many examples of the clout followers can have. During the 1989 Velvet Revolution in Czechoslovakia, a most spectacular and sudden uprising took place. Just a week after the fall of the Berlin Wall, students gathered in Prague. The police crackdown was fierce, but this only galvanised the protesters. The following days saw demonstrations of up to half a million people. In late November the communist leadership agreed to relinquish its power and democratic elections were held in June of the following year.

Followers can be powerful when they join together, either with the leader, in support of the leader or to follow their own hopes and dreams. *People Power* manifests on large and small scales and can be instrumental in the effectiveness of the leader.

NEW LEADERS

When leadership changes occur in animal societies, the group will often suffer a period of upheaval and insecurity. Leadership changes at the top can be disruptive. When a CEO announces he or she is moving on it can leave employees with much trepidation as to who the new leader might be and what changes they might bring. Followers will have had either good or bad experiences under the previous regime and that will shape their expectations of the new leader. Like us, animals feel their world shakes when there are big changes at the top.

New leaders can take a little while in finding their feet. From being 'one of the herd' to taking on the leadership can be a huge responsibility. In the case of Przewalski's Horse, also known as the Takhi or Mongolian Wild Horse, a stallion leader takes his harem to food and water and protects the females and their foals. Pascale Benoit, the senior ungulate (animals with hooves) keeper in Taronga Western Plains Zoo witnessed some leadership lessons learned by a relatively inexperienced stallion Przewalski's Horse:

'Stallion Nicolai was a first-time father and became very protective of one mare in particular once she had his foal. He tried to keep all the other females in the herd at a distance from her, shooing them away. He did not understand the concept of a harem and having to look after *all* his mares. He started being horrible to the rest of his herd.

This went on for about three weeks before the lead mare, Gengis, and her helper took him on. The two high-ranking mares obviously thought he was being a threat to the other mares and foals within the herd. His behaviour was threatening the cohesion of the harem and the foals were in danger due to his kicks. Gengis and her second-ranking collaborator drafted him away from the group and let him have it. They gave him a good hiding. Something they would also have done to a stallion in the wild if he was not up to the job. From that moment onwards, Nicolai's whole attitude changed. He got the message. A stallion is meant to keep his harem together at all times. He is meant to protect them and their foals from another stallion coming in and taking over. After his 'lesson' from the high-ranking mares in the group, Nicolai is now the stallion he was born to be.'

Nicolai's followers set him straight. In many social animal societies there are ways that the followers influence the kind of leadership they want. Some animal leaders seem more in tune with what they are meant to do as new leaders than Nicolai was. Jo Richardson, a zoo husbandry veteran, now at Wellington Zoo Trust, New Zealand, relates her experience of introducing an inexperienced young new male Lion to the leadership role:

'Many years ago, in Europe, I worked with a Lion pride: a male with four lionesses. When the male was first introduced to this female pride he was not the most confident as he was still quite young. He had to establish himself as leader in a group of strongly bonded sibling females – no easy task as the lionesses were confident individuals and very territorial. The male, Leon, must have realised that his way into leadership was not to force an altercation with the group but to assert his authority over each female as an individual, one at a time. Leon found his feet quite quickly using this approach. He was accepted by the females and the pride was successful.'

People who are new to leadership need to get a good understanding of what the followers expect from them. A different approach may be needed for each follower, as Lion Leon understood. Stallion Nicolai was out of his depth in his new role, but was soon to accept the 'correction' by the alpha mares. Both the herd and Nicolai benefitted from that intervention.

What can we learn from these animal examples?
• Be brave as a new leader and take the time to learn the job.
• Put the greater good of the team ahead of personal gain.
• Accept feedback from the team.
• Recognise the team as individuals.

DEPOSED LEADERS

What happens to deposed leaders? They can isolate themselves and suffer the lack of emotional support that the group can offer them, or they can still hang out with the other high-ranking animals but in a lower status position. Some will be able to create a bond with the new alpha and become a powerful influencer behind the throne. Others will hang on for too long and lose support over time.

In the animal world it is often only during the leader's peak performance years that he or she has the endurance for the alpha role. Robert Sapolsky studied Savanna Baboons for many years and comments on the fall from the alpha position by male Solomon:

'Solomon did not merely trade places with Uriah, becoming number two in the hierarchy. He had maintained the alpha position long past the point when he had the physical means to do so, holding on purely by dint of status quo and intimidation. Solomon's rank plummeted to ninth position, solidly in the middle of the group. A pattern emerged that has grown familiar to me over the years. Once the tables are turned, baboons are endowed with long, vengeful memories. Solomon got no end of grief.'

Leadership changes in animal groups can also happen smoothly but only if the deposed leader and followers both accept the changes at the top. Sometimes the followers influence the change, sometimes they just support it and get on with life. One such example is described by Harmony Neale who has looked after the Chimpanzees in Wellington Zoo Trust in New Zealand for fourteen years. During that time there have been two different male leaders. When Harmony started, Marty had just taken over leadership from his brother. More recently, male Alexis has taken over the alpha position from Marty.

'Marty now is thirty-two years old and was the alpha male for about sixteen years, which is a long time to be in such a demanding position. Alexis the new alpha male, at twenty years, is at a perfect age to rule. Marty was a very laid-back and easy-going leader. As he got older he probably lost a bit of his confidence in dealing with the young males. The community would support him if he had to assert his dominance but he probably let those young males get away with a bit more than before. Marty always had very good support from the females – they were there to back him up.

Alexis is also a fairly laid-back leader and has now been in the alpha position for about eighteen months. When he was growing up you could always see traits in him showing that he would be a good leader one day. He was one of the first chimps that the females would allow their baby to go to. He was always very caring with the youngsters, would be there to comfort them, always wanted to know what they were doing and be a back-up for them.

He was always a very caring chimp. He would share food and groom the females. The change in leadership between Marty and Alexis was gradual. There had been an earthquake and Marty was very much on-edge but still functioning. He was, however, hesitant to come inside the building at night. The leadership challenge would have happened anyway but Alexis saw his opportunity at this time, possibly thinking: 'Well, Marty isn't around as much so I am going to step in.' Marty stood aside and let Alexis take over; we always thought he would. It got to the point where he was ready to step down and let someone else take control.

The females took a little time to accept that Alexis was now the leader. It took a while for the girls to stop looking at Marty for support. When they were upset and looked for consolation, Marty would show them: 'No, you don't come to me anymore.' They would then have to go to Alexis to get that support. Alexis, being twenty years old, still has those testosterone outbursts that teenage chimps can have. If Alexis oversteps the mark, Marty won't get involved but the females will. If he goes too far, the females seem to say: 'No you don't do that, this is unacceptable in this group.' He then looks a little sheepish for the rest of the day and the next day it is all settled down.

Alexis is now firmly in place as the alpha male and has a signature dominancy display; he likes to use props and bang them with his hands or feet. Marty is number two in the hierarchy and the community of ten chimps has settled around its new leader.'

Leadership changes resulting in loss of power and status can hit hard for someone who is used to being an 'important person'. A good leader who is deposed, demoted or who has lost the election could learn from Chimpanzee Marty. Marty showed grace in defeat. He showed his support for the new leader and retained the powerful, respected position of a high-ranking elder. If Marty had not accepted the change, he could have undermined Alexis's position by allowing the females to come to him for consolation or in other ways. Undermining actions or regular challenges by a deposed leader bring instability to the group.

When animals lose power, they can be either like Marty or like Solomon. There is a choice. Leaders can exit gracefully and maintain respect or they can hold on to power by intimidation for too long and lose all the influence they had. In our societies, in politics in particular, we do not always see a graceful exit by a deposed leader. They may have lost the top job but they are not willing to let go of power. In business, new leaders may also find this type of opposition when they start their new job. Perhaps someone has tried for the role or has held it in an acting capacity during the recruitment process but was not ultimately selected. This can be a difficult situation for a new leader. In these circumstances, it may be wise to work out if some power or face-saving can be offered to a deposed leader if it would help to bring harmony to the team. In the Chimpanzee world a new alpha may work in alliance with such a male, at least until he has wider group support.

CONSOLATION IS A ROLE OF LEADERSHIP

A scared Chimpanzee looks for comfort from another chimp. When frightened they will run to someone who may comfort them. Often, the leader is one who gives consolation. Similarly, when we receive bad news or are scared, a hug, even from a stranger, is of great comfort. Consoling the people in your care is a leadership task. Our political leaders are there when there's a natural disaster, a plane crash, flood or other calamity. Their role is to console. They are on the news to vocalise the grief, shock and concern the nation feels. The role of consoler is very important in leadership and must not be handed to an assistant to 'send flowers' and be done with. Personal attention in traumatic situations is what matters most and is an important aspect of leadership.

THE ROLE OF FOLLOWERS IN LEADERSHIP CHALLENGES

Many of my observations on this topic are based on the Chimpanzees in their large open-air habitat at Taronga Zoo in Sydney, where I have worked for some three decades. Over this time chimps were born and died or arrived from or were sent to other zoos. The chimp group was always big, anywhere between seventeen and thirty-two individuals. Many of the chimps were related to each other, mother and adult sons being a well-represented combination. There were several changes of leadership within the group and subsequent changes in the ranking of other group members. If a leading male lost his position, the ranking of his immediate family could go down also.

One morning when the keepers arrived there was a subdued atmosphere in the chimp night-house. We had to take Lubutu to the dentist – well, the dentist comes to Lubutu. He had lost a couple of canine teeth in a fight with a male called Chimbuka. Chimbuka had an injury to his face which could have been caused by a canine tooth, so it was not difficult to work out what had happened. Some dominance struggle had happened during the night and it seemed that Lubutu had won. Now we had a problem. We would have to take Lubutu out to get his broken canines fixed. The challenging male would have the opportunity to plot to overthrow Lubutu upon his return.

Lubutu would need an anaesthetic and was likely to be groggy afterwards. There would be no fair fight if there was to be one. The answer was to separate the two potential rivals with their family and supporters in different parts of the chimp night-house. Lubutu could then recover in another part in peace. Once everything had settled down, Lubutu and Chimbuka were reunited and keepers could carefully observe how the reconciliation progressed. Chimpanzees are very good at making up after fights. Often the older females play a big role in making sure the males reconcile, often literally bringing them back together to make up after a fight so that peace can be restored. There was a lot of tension in the group once all the males were in the same space again. We kept close watch to see who was grooming whom as an indication of reconciliatory moves. Once again, the females proved their political power in the group. They clearly showed their support for Lubutu by gathering around him and grooming him exclusively. Chimbuka got the hint. As they say in politics, he realised he 'did not have the numbers'. Grooming in chimps is an important statement: other chimps know what it signifies.

In our own culture, the support of followers impacts a leader's reputation. If the leader is liked and respected by the team, they are likely in turn to get better support from those directly above them. In human terms, this can result in increased budgets, improved opportunities and more challenging work.

FEMALE FOLLOWER POWER IN GORILLAS

In Western Lowland Gorillas, despite strong authoritarian leadership, sometimes the followers take control. Despite the lack of real cohesion between the females, they too will band together occasionally to tell their leader off if he's overstepped the mark.

Melissa Shipway, an experienced great ape keeper, remembers

when the Taronga gorilla females would gang up on their authoritarian leader:

'Normally Kibabu was good at resolving conflict between his females. Just his presence was enough. He would move to position himself right in the middle of the conflict. That would make them all take a step back. Just Kibabu standing there for a moment was enough to settle any dispute.'

But occasionally Kibabu himself would be the target of a confrontation.

'About every six months or so there would be an altercation with his group. He'd obviously done something wrong but we could never work out what it was that he'd done. The females would clump together facing him, all uttering a bloodcurdling scream. Then they would step it up a notch and chase him. It was quite amusing actually to see the big fellow running for his life and all his females chasing after him. The kids would usually join in as well – it really was the whole group against the silverback. For whatever reason, he knew that he was in the doghouse and never retaliated. He would just take it, move away and keep himself out of sight for a couple of days. Female Kriba was often the instigator, and Mouila and Frala would follow her lead. We don't know what the precursors were. That's the problem with gorillas – their behaviour is so subtle that you miss many cues. We see it with new male Kibali too when he's done something not so favourable. The females will band together and put him in his place.'

Even under the leadership of a strong authoritarian, the followers will rise up in protest if the leader gets it very wrong. Clearly, the lesson we can take here from the animal world is that followers have limits which even controlling leaders cannot ignore. Not overstepping the mark and keeping followers contented is a good strategy for leadership longevity.

STRESS AT THE TOP AND AT THE BOTTOM OF THE HIERARCHY

Changing a primate's social standing can significantly impact its wellbeing. A low-ranking animal gets picked on and will likely suffer stress. A top-ranking animal can also be under a lot of stress to maintain the alpha status. Studies looking at Savanna Baboons found that high-stress hormones were equally present in both the alpha males and males at the lower levels of the hierarchy. For males at the lower end of the hierarchy, the stress may be associated with limited access to resources. For males at the top, the stress comes from antagonistic interactions with other males. For health and wellbeing, animals and people might on the whole be better off being in the middle to top rank without reaching the alpha position.

LEADERSHIP CULTURE

We tend to think that the way a particular species is led is more or less fixed, but external factors can bring change. An interesting example of cultural leadership change in primates is given by Robert Sapolsky and his colleague and wife, Lisa Share.

Sapolsky, a primatologist, studied Savanna Baboons from the late 1970s until 1986, when a tuberculosis outbreak selectively killed off the most aggressive males in a group he was studying, which he called 'The Forest Troop'. Baboon leadership is naturally quite violent. But how much is hardwired and how much is culture? The victims of the disease outbreak in Sapolsky's group had been the top male leaders. They had been strong enough to fight the neighbouring clan for the infected meat on the garbage dump of an irresponsible tourist lodge. Sapolsky had to give up his study and didn't return to the area for ten years.

When he did come back he found drastic changes in the behaviour of the troop. Tuberculosis had killed the most dominant males and those left were the low-ranking males, females and their young. This major change in demographics brought a cultural shift towards a more peaceable society, evidenced by a more relaxed dominance hierarchy. Males were fighting less, sat closer together and groomed one another, even though they still scrapped occasionally – they are baboons after all. Remarkably, though, this observable change in aggression levels continued two decades later despite the turnover of males during this time. The Forest Troop females must have liked the new order of things and found a way of instructing incoming males in the new moral code of the troop. A change in the leadership culture is more likely to happen when a new leader takes over from an old leader, but at other times it can happen purely on the basis of demographics. If the composition of the team changes from dominance by one gender to a predominance of the other gender, things can change rapidly.

These changes may have happened because the now-predominant female gender balance was able to instruct the young incoming males who had not yet learned to be overly aggressive.

Frans de Waal also observed a change in the culture of leadership in the Bonobo troop in San Diego Zoo (see Chapter 10). The troop was run by male Vernon and only housed one single female, Loretta. At that time it was not universally known that Bonobo society is essentially matriarchal. Once another female arrived the natural order of the Bonobo world was restored. Loretta became the leader of the group, supported by only one female companion and Vernon now had to be submissive to the new rulers who controlled the food supply. It took only one minor change in the make-up of the group to alter the leadership culture from male to female dominated. New leadership cultures can develop, for better or for worse, if group structure or other influencing factors change.

In animal groups cultural change can be slow, but when caring for animals in a zoo situation we can sometimes influence cultural leadership by initiating changes in either leaders or followers. To do so, we may add more of one gender or the other to a group. We might move the animals to a new enclosure where perhaps 'ownership' of toys or favourite spots to sit have to be re-established. The introduction to the new spot or toy and the order in which it happens can influence who may become more dominant. If a particular group gets to the new environment first, this can influence who may feel more empowered to take charge. If a particular group gets to spend time together before the rest arrives this can influence the culture in the new place too. Alliances can then develop away from other influences and influencers. I am inclined to believe that all these options would be just as potentially useful in the human context as they are in baboons, Chimpanzees or Bonobos.

WHY COALITIONS MATTER

Coalitions are powerful tools in social animals and people. Coalitions can make or break leaders, and they result in negative and positive outcomes. Understanding how coalitions form in the animal world, and in chimps in particular, may be worthwhile for human leaders. Chimp males can be rivals in one year and allies in the next, depending on who needs whose support to do what. Some alpha male chimps are very forceful when it comes to breaking up coalitions. Grooming creates bonds between individual animals and bonds lead to alliances which can be political and used for power. Frodo, one of Jane Goodall's observed chimps, would charge any accumulation of grooming males and break up the bonding session just in case they were plotting against him. He was an alpha male several times but only for a short time on each occasion. Frodo failed to grasp some of the more subtle tools of power.

Some chimps, however, are particularly good at using their alliances for their own benefit. Frans de Waal in his book *Peacemaking Among Primates* retells a story by Japanese Chimpanzee researcher Toshisada Nishida:

'An old male in the Mahale group regularly changed sides between two younger males who each needed the old male's support in order to dominate the other. Nishida, who was able to keep track of the fighting males in the jungle for several months, speaks of 'allegiance fickleness'. In this way the old male created a key role for himself, one that paid off in sexual privileges.'

Alliances and bonding are key in chimp communities from an early age. Male chimps don't leave the natal group. It is therefore really important that they find their ranking or position in the group. This may be influenced by their mother and her ranking but also by who they align themselves with. For a male chimp, this is the group he is going to spend his entire life with. For young subordinate chimps, the decision of who to befriend and support is a tricky one. If this friend becomes a high-ranking chimp, their status and ranking will rise too. If they support an individual who gets into trouble with the alpha, they too may suffer. Supporting other individuals in the group can therefore be a risk. *Choose your friends wisely*, we would say.

To avoid any kind of incest, female chimps join a neighbouring group once they become sexually mature. They then need to find their place in the new troop. Female chimps in human care, even more so than wild chimps, will also develop a strong hierarchy and deep friendships. These relationships are usually more stable than male chimp friendships. Females who give birth around the same time have babies and toddlers at the same time. Those two youngsters want to play together and as a result, the mothers spend a lot of time together too, not unlike the way we form mothers' groups and playgroups. They end up sitting together, grooming each other and deep friendships can result.

Good leaders in our world form coalitions too but perhaps they don't always see them as that. Together a leader and their followers can achieve amazing things when energy doesn't have to spend on leadership struggles. Energy spent on bringing leaders and followers together, however, is an investment in the future. Every time I see a chimp groom another, I know that chimp is making an investment in group cohesion and solidarity. The more support a leader has, the more likely it is that his or her vision will come to fruition. A leader has to spend time with their team, whether that is around the water cooler or after work at the pub, or a quick coffee before a meeting – these times are important bonding opportunities and are how trust develops and alliances built.

IT'S ALL ABOUT THE FOLLOWERS

It is apparent that leadership relies on knowing what's in it for the followers. Good leaders connect with their team. They understand the individual needs of team members and make them feel valued for their contribution. Validated, nurtured people in the workplace can achieve great things together and make the world a better place. Woe betide the leader who neglects their followers. In my decades of observing animal leaders, self-serving leaders have never had a happy ending.

Great leaders:
- Recognise the power of their followers.
- Invest time in bonding with the team.
- Demonstrate their values and share vision to get team 'buy-in'.
- Care about the individuals that make up the team so they feel nurtured and protected.

• Reconcile conflict, both between followers and between followers and themselves.

Leaders and followers that are mutually supportive will be more likely to have a positive atmosphere at work, be more productive, suffer less stress, have less staff turnover and live healthier, happier lives. The animal world shows us that leaders have to demonstrate their values, share their vision and care about the individuals they lead if they wish to stay in the alpha position.

HOW DO OLD MOBILE PHONES HELP THE GREAT APES IN AFRICA?

Coltan is a mineral used in the creation of mobile phones and its mining results in the clearance of habitat in Africa where Chimpanzees, Bonobos and gorillas live. Miners also contribute to the bushmeat trade, by opening roads in the bush that let the poachers in, further accelerating the decline of great ape populations.

By removing mobile phones from the waste stream the impact of mining on great apes is reduced. Many zoos in Australia and elsewhere have recycling projects for mobile phones. Dr Zanna Clay, research expert and conservationist for Bonobos, says: 'Unsustainable and unregulated mining of coltan poses a direct threat to the surrounding forest ecosystems in Democratic Republic of Congo, an area rich in biodiversity and home to thousands of endemic species, including Bonobos and Chimpanzees, our closest living relatives. Without effective regulation in place, coltan mines have become a hotbed of human rights violations, including large-scale levels of child slavery and horrendous working conditions. By recycling your mobile phone, you are helping to support the fight against these human rights violations, as well as reducing the high-demand for a mineral which is degrading the natural richness of Congo as we speak.'

By simply recycling an old mobile phone, the pressure on great ape habitats is reduced whilst some programs use the money raised from refurbished handsets to support great ape conservation in central Africa.

CHAPTER 12
NATURAL LEADERSHIP

'Why should our nastiness be the baggage of an apish past and our kindness uniquely human? Why should we not seek continuity with other animals for our 'noble' traits as well?'

STEPHEN JAY GOULD

From the laissez-faire Lion to maternalistic elephants, wild animal leadership is varied, covering a spectrum from autocratic to democratic. Each leadership style evolved to maximise the success of each species in surviving and thriving in their natural environment and in adapting to changes in that environment over time. We, too, have evolved with a social structure and leadership style that has served our species well in the past. But perhaps our circumstances have changed faster than our brains have adapted, as discussed in Chapter 3. Some of the expectations we have of our leaders are a specific response to cultural changes. But these can be hard to separate from the expectations that are hardwired in us as social animals. Those hardwired expectations, likely dating from our prehistoric origins, match closely to the leadership needs of our animal cousins.

In this chapter we take another close look at our primate cousins, their societies and their leadership styles. Bonobos and chimps represent the Yin and Yang of human nature, like having two first cousins, equally closely related but very different from each other. Together, the behaviour of these two great apes seems to reflect our own ruthless, aggressive side (chimps) and our more egalitarian, peace-loving natures (Bonobos).

This chapter therefore aims to answer the questions:

What lessons from the animal world are relevant to human leaders today?

How should leaders act in a way that satisfies our evolutionary expectations of leadership?

Each of the animal leadership styles examined in the previous chapters tells us something about leadership models that work well in nature. Which of the positive qualities in those models could or should we emulate? The negative traits in those leadership styles speak for themselves: examples of animal leaders who monopolised resources like food and sex and used violence and intimidation to seize or stay in power have already been given. In my three decades of experience I observed that it *never* ended well for those types of leaders. It's far more instructive to focus on the positive traits that animal leaders display that result in long-lasting and thriving animal teams.

POSITIVE TRAITS IN WILD LEADERS

The African great apes are particularly relevant to understanding how our love of hierarchy has evolved. Each of these great apes has a different model of hierarchy. Gorillas have a harem system whereby the all-powerful male is in complete charge and the females are not very bonded to each other. Chimpanzee troops are male dominated, with an alpha in alliance with other powerful males whilst chimp females use their coalitions to counterbalance male power. Lastly, we have female-dominated Bonobo troops, where older alpha females are in control. Our natural hierarchies in western society might lean more towards the chimp model, but there are aspects of each of these primate social structures reflected in ours.

Both Bonobos and Chimpanzees use complex leadership strategies to maintain social harmony in the group. These strategies give us insights into dealing with the pressure and stress of group living. Complex ape societies work best if the leaders try to minimise harm to the clan by keeping the peace. What counts is that the clan is cohesive and collaborates when it really matters, such as in times of danger.

We have seen that patterns emerge across the different animal leadership styles, emerging in what leaders and their followers find important, and how this translates into the success of the community as a whole.

• Primates, like us, have innate expectations of our leaders.

• We want a leader who we can trust.

• We want a leader who has our back and makes us feel safe because of the challenges inherent in conflict resolution and security.

- We want a leader who is competent and benevolent and who acquires resources and shares them.

We, along with the other African great apes, evolved to expect our leaders to display the kind of behaviours that deliver on these expectations of leadership. Our political, religious and business leaders should all be aware of this 'social contract' we have regarding leadership and they should act accordingly. Understanding these innate expectations will make leadership feel more natural and potentially more rewarding for those willing to lead.

A LEADER WHOM WE CAN TRUST

Trustworthiness is the number one desirable trait in a wild animal leader. The troop or clan wants to be able to *trust* their leader. The silverback gorilla is willing to fight to the death to defend his troop and we, too, expect leaders in whom we have placed our trust to always have our best interests at heart. This trust in our leader is what allows us to feel safe. Teenage female Bonobos joining a new group seek the support and protection of an older high-ranking female in the new troop, just as we might place our trust in an older colleague or experienced leader in a new company.

Abraham Maslow developed a theory of human motivation, now often referred to as Maslow's Hierarchy of Needs. In his book *Psychological Review*, published in 1943, Maslow proposed that a human's first needs were physiological – food, water, shelter and so on. Once these needs were satisfied, the next priority is safety. After that comes belonging and love, esteem, self-actualisation and self-transcendence. This theory, while sometimes criticised, still has widespread influence outside academia. It also closely resembles my understanding of the demands of animals in human care, namely that their physical, behavioural and intellectual needs must all be met for them to thrive.

As we have discussed in the previous chapters, our most basic instincts play a role in how safe or valued we feel. Feeling safe determines how much we trust the leader. This in turn influences how willing we are to follow that leader. The leader we *want* to follow inspires trust and loyalty and has an understanding of our innate emotional and social needs.

As a zookeeper, you develop very close relationships with your fellow keepers and veterinarians. Like co-parenting, you all care deeply for the creatures you jointly look after. You also perform some potentially dangerous tasks together, like catching animals that could kill or harm you if mistakes are made. When you give an injection to a venomous snake you really have to trust the person who is holding its head! Or when catching a sick and stranded Leopard Seal on the beach, several people have to hold the animal down, and trust in the leader's decision about who grabs which bit and the timing thereof is crucial. In jobs like zookeeping, your wellbeing or even your life may depend on trusting the skills of others. But this develops only after you have had multiple experiences as a team and when colleagues have proven that trust is warranted. Trust in the workplace, and in animal societies alike, creates harmony. Without trust we are less happy and more open to worry and fear. Every interaction can build trust, but it takes time to develop and can be lost in an instant.

Leaders are people too. Where we are in the hierarchy does not change our need for approval and support. Leaders need to feel safe with their followers. Trust is a two-way street and must go both ways to create and maintain a happy and productive workplace.

WE WANT A LEADER WHO HAS OUR BACK AND MAKE US FEEL SAFE

There are leaders we want to follow for their admirable qualities and there are leaders who are followed reluctantly because they use aggression and intimidation tactics. Trusted leaders only need to use the appropriate amount of control to manage their team. Chimpanzee leaders who overuse aggression to maintain power will create a group filled with fear. As a result, the alpha's alliances may break down and his previous supporters may plot to overthrow him, creating instability in the troop. On the other hand, *underuse* of power can also lead to instability. If teenager chimps are not corrected when they overstep social norms or when quarrels between individuals are not resolved, the group's harmony will also dissolve.

Jo Richardson, now at Wellington Zoo Trust, New Zealand, has spent her career working with eight different communities of Chimpanzees. In Jo's experience:

'Alpha Chimpanzee males that use bully tactics to run the community usually do not stay in that position very long. They are usually overthrown within a couple of years. The bully asserts his dominance often through force, which the community will only put up with for a short while. As soon as there is a suitable up-and-coming male who shows a more diplomatic approach, the rest of the community will get behind him and overthrow the bully using political allegiances.'

People working directly with wild animals will come up with the same reasons again and again for why some animal leaders succeed or fail. Jane Goodall's research on Chimpanzees in Gombe National Park confirms that a popular, considered alpha may be able to hang on to the top job for much longer, while an aggressive and harrying leader may only be able to stay in his position for a couple of years.

Despite the danger involved in leaving the protection of the social group, many animals will choose to leave a 'bad leader' and take their chances of finding a new group. Human workers too, will often chose to leave a despotic leader. Research by Mark van Vugt and colleagues found that attrition rates were four times greater in autocratically led groups than in those led democratically.

CHIMP LANGUAGE

Humans can learn other languages and some find it easier than others. It was assumed that animals do not have control over the sounds they make due to a different brain structure. This has long been held up as an example of the uniqueness of humans. It now seems that this assumption is not correct. Animals produce vocalisations that refer to objects in their environment. For example, Meerkats differentiate their calls to warn others of an aerial predator or a terrestrial predator. Primates also have a range of vocalisations that refer to various objects in their environment. A group of chimps moved from the Netherlands to Edinburgh Zoo. Researchers studied their vocalisations before and after the move to their new home. Three years later, the recordings show that that the 'Dutch' chimps had begun vocalising words like 'apple' the same way as the 'Scottish' chimps did.

'The assumption has been that animals do not have control over the sounds they make, whereas we socially learn the labels for things – which is what separates us from animals', says Katie Slocombe of the University of York, UK. 'The important thing we've now shown is that, with the food calls, they changed the structure to fit in with their new group members, so the Dutch calls for 'apple' changed to the Edinburgh ones,' says Slocombe, 'It's the first time call structure has been dissociated from emotional outbursts.'

BUILDING AND KEEPING ALLIANCES

As we have seen, a popular chimp leader will be able to rule for longer than an unpopular one. However, a new chimp leader does not get there by himself. He has allies that support him in overthrowing the alpha male. His job as the new leader is then to nurture coalitions to maintain his position. Building power alliances is a political strategy that requires considerable cognitive abilities. Yet, it is most likely that the common ancestor of humans and the other great apes used alliances millions of years ago to gain control and dominance before we separated into different species. Alliance building for dominance is therefore a strategy that evolution tells us is advantageous.

Many other species also use this tried and tested way of retaining control. Spotted Hyenas or Bonobos for example would not be able to run their matriarchies if it wasn't for the females' coalition.

In Chimpanzee males there is a strong motivator to seek power; power equals access to females for sex. Subordinate males want that too and are constantly on the lookout for chinks in the alpha's armour. This can lead to ongoing undermining of the leader so another can take over. Challengers will often rally allies first, just like politicians counting the number of supporters they have before challenging the leader. Chimps will put on a good dominance display, aiming to intimidate the alpha, and they may perform mock attacks to see how many supporters come to their aid as opposed to the aid of the alpha.

Building alliances takes time. Chimpanzee and Bonobo societies are all about giving and calling in favours. Grooming, sexual favours, food sharing and supporting one another during quarrels are all highly valued favours. The savvy ape knows exactly what his or her score is with each individual in the group. The more socially aware an ape is, the more likely this is reflected in the individual's ranking in the hierarchy.

Jo Richardson, chimp expert, believes that social awareness and good leadership in chimps is about adaptability. The alpha has to adapt to his environment, but he also has to adapt his personality and leadership style to the community and each individual within that group. He has to make decisions for the greater good of the chimp troop.

'What I have seen in chimp communities in the wild and in human care is that good chimp leaders have the ability to take on board each individual character within that community but can also make decisions that ensure the community's safety and ability to succeed.'

Skilful alphas do favours for everybody, share food, groom and use this as a way of showing fairness. Close allies will perhaps receive more favours than others, but this is always judged by how much is needed to keep them on side. In human terms we should take care to reward our people as evenly as possible, although at times it may be necessary to praise an insecure person more than a really confident one. Opportunities for advancement, gaining experience at the more interesting tasks, the chance for perks and rewards should be equally available to everyone in the group. Despite the need to keep everyone on side, an effective alpha chimp would not turn a blind eye to misbehaviour in the group, however, and nor should human leaders. Ignoring misdemeanours, particularly from high-ranking members of the team, is demoralising for the rest and can lead to discontent with the leader.

It is also apparent that the bigger the coalitions are, the stronger the power base. We too need to build networks of support in our lives at work, at home and in our communities. These alliance networks need constant maintenance. Complacency, taking support for granted, is the downfall of many an alpha, in human as well as in ape communities.

GIFT GIVING AND SHARING

Humans give each other little gifts occasionally. Chimps and Bonobos do the same in the form of food sharing. These actions help to cement relationships. A small gift to a colleague for their birthday, for example, or after helping out with a difficult task. In a similar vein, chimps do social favours for one another. The group members know exactly what favours they have performed and which they have received. There appears to be social obligation, a moral obligation, to reciprocate favours. If a chimp has supported a friend during an altercation with another chimp, they will expect support next time they themselves are in a fight and need a friend. Not to do so would damage Chimpanzee friendships.

FEMALE COALITIONS

Bonobo females are the main coalition in their matriarchal social structure, but females in a male-led chimp group have their own hierarchy too. At the time of writing, the dominant female in the Taronga troop is Lisa. She is a leader in a powerful group of females. Without the support of the female powerbase, the alpha, Lubutu, would struggle to maintain his position. It's important to note that none of these females would be strong enough to stand up to a male alone, but together they are a force to be reckoned with. Female chimps in zoos in particular have strong bonds and join forces to set a misbehaving male straight. They support other females when they meet with male aggression. They confiscate weapons from males. They make males come together after altercations and make them reconcile. They frequently use their collective power to limit the dominance of a male. They are known to play 'king maker' by showing their support for an alpha or his challenger.

Female gorillas, despite their lack of strong bonds with each other, will also occasionally gang up on a male. We saw this at Taronga when Kriba, Mouila and Frala beat up on Kibabu when he was not up to the job. Coalitions are crucial for matriarchal species, such as the Spotted Hyena. No leader in nature can lead without followers. Followers have power and many know just how to use it. The human equivalent, I always think, can be seen in the power of unions and professional associations. On their own, a worker has little bargaining power, but united they have influence and authority. Successful leaders know how to keep their followers and supporters on side.

THE INFLUENCE OF THE ELDERS

In primate societies, it is not only the alpha male who is influential. Subject to personality, the oldest male and oldest female are often very influential animals in the group. The elder statesmen and stateswomen are the ones who can calm down an irate alpha male or make two fighting males stop and make up. They can play a big role in the group with regards to reconciliation and cohesion.

We see this a lot in world politics also. Often a president, prime minister or senior minister who is no longer in power still wields considerable clout in the public domain and possibly behind closed doors in the 'corridors of power'.

CONFLICT RESOLUTION AND CONSOLATION

Conflict is inevitable in social animals, including people. How the conflict is resolved is the key to group cohesion. One of the reasons we have leaders is to resolve tension in our communities. We need someone to be a respected arbiter of disputes. Someone we trust has to make sure that conflict does not simmer and undermine the unity of the clan. Resolving conflict is such an important task that it strongly influences the success of an alpha. Empathy, standing up for the weak and protecting the vulnerable are qualities we admire in leaders, be they human or ape. This increases trust in them. A bullying leader might not be tolerated, but nor will a leader who turns a blind eye to conflict.

As we saw in Chapter 9, Chimpanzee Lubutu was reluctant to intervene in any clashes in the group when he first became a leader. As he grew older and bigger, the females made it clear to him that his reluctance to resolve conflict was no longer an option.

Dominant chimps will often support the weaker animal against the stronger. Of course, sometimes conflicts are resolved by the alpha by not taking one side against another. As the alpha, the more noble position to take is to not spring to the defence of your friends but rather to bring peace to the community. Lubutu, the alpha chimp in Taronga Zoo, knows this now and has learned many strategies in dealing with conflict.

In Bonobos too, conflict resolution is an important attribute of good leadership. Young Bonobo females being harassed by males will be supported by the older females to bring the males under control. This helps the bonding between members of the sisterhood.

Chimps embrace, kiss and make up, while Bonobos have sex and make up! Chimps and Bonobos are both very good at reconciling after fights. This need to resolve conflict is an emotional driver in people too. Sometimes we lay awake at night, worrying about a conflict we've had that still needs to be resolved. We are genetically predisposed to restoring social harmony. A true leader sorts out disagreements fairly, swiftly and effectively without the need for too much aggression.

SOCIAL BELONGING

Leaders who spend time with their team can create more cohesion and an increased sense of belonging in the group. Chimp Lubutu makes sure he spends time with his male allies, grooms the females, plays with the babies and hangs out with the teenage boys. Kibabu, the gorilla silverback, similarly spends time with his harem and plays with the infants. Bonobos live in close contact, grooming and sharing food. Leaders in wild animal societies know the individuals they lead. Many animals have rituals to reinforce this bonding. In the case of African Wild Dogs, this may be excited greetings each time they reunite after a short absence, or the animated embracing and kissing of Chimpanzees and Bonobos when they greet one another. All these rituals say: 'You matter to me, we are kin.' Animals and humans all need to feel that they belong in their clan. A leader must create a group culture for that feeling of belonging to thrive.

WE WANT A LEADER WHO IS COMPETENT AND BENEVOLENT

There are some recurring patterns in what is most valued by the animal groups we have discussed in previous chapters. Male dominated societies tend to revolve around sex and power. Female dominated societies put food and the safety of offspring at the fore.

Some chimp alphas are tolerant of other males mating with oestrus females, but many are not. Subordinate males often get their chance to mate out of the alpha's view. Female-led Bonobos, however, allow everybody access to sex so there is no competition for it that can lead to conflict. But even in male-led primate societies, what followers want is a leader competent enough to provide resources to the troop. He must make sure that the territory is large enough to supply sufficient food, water and opportunities to reproduce, and he must be benevolent enough to share these relatively equitably.

In human societies, this is not always the case. Even in countries that are affluent enough to feed their people, the distribution of wealth is not exactly fair and equitable. In our western democracies, 1 per cent of the people take nearly a quarter of the nation's income. In terms of wealth rather than income, the top 1 per cent control 40 per cent. The top 1 per cent have the best houses, the best education, the best doctors, and the best lifestyles, but there is one thing that money doesn't seem to have bought: an understanding that their fate is bound up with how the other 99 per cent live. Throughout history, this is something that the top 1 per cent eventually do learn but often too late. The desire for equitable sharing in western society was highlighted by the Occupy Wall Street (OWS) movement, which began in September 2011. Protestors occupied Zuccotti Park in New York City's Wall Street financial district. The protest received global attention for the issue of economic inequality, financial greed and corruption worldwide. The OWS slogan, 'We are the 99 per cent' refers to the income inequality and wealth distribution in the US between the wealthiest 1 per cent and the rest of the population. When the protestors were forced out of Zuccotti Park they turned to occupying banks, corporate headquarters and university campuses. The *Chicago Tribune*, in an article measuring the impacts from this protest five years on, draws the following conclusion: OWS takes some credit for introducing income inequality into the broader political discourse, for inspiring the fight for a US$15 minimum wage and for creating a receptive audience for the Democratic presidential campaign of Senator Bernie Sanders.

The protest changed public debate and inspired a generation of activists. In primate communities and human ones, this is what we expect from our leaders; fair sharing of the resources. Leaders that do not distribute the resources fairly through equal pay or support will find it difficult to maintain support of the followers.

Sarah Brosnan and Frans de Waal conducted a trial illustrating fairness in capuchin monkeys. They played a game with these small South American primates where each monkey was given a pebble and if they returned it they received a piece of cucumber in exchange. Capuchins learn this game quickly because cucumber is better than a pebble. Once the capuchins were familiar with the game an unfair concept was introduced. Two monkeys who had been sitting side-by-side, happily exchanging pebbles for cucumber 25 times in row, were now inequitably treated, with one of the monkeys receiving a grape for his pebble while the other continued to receive cucumber. The cucumber receiver noticed her neighbour was getting nice juicy grapes (much more interesting than cucumber) and became so upset that she started to throw the pebbles and cucumber back at the researchers. Cucumber had been fine until she noticed that someone was getting a much better reward for the same work.

Monkeys know when something is unfair and so do we. These experiments have now been conducted with dogs, birds, Chimpanzees and other species. It looks like no species likes unfairness.

THE LEADERSHIP WE WANT

In previous chapters we looked at the different leadership styles of several mammal species from Lions and elephants to Meerkats and Bonobos. Each species has adopted a leadership model that works in their society. In a human context, we don't need to use a single model but have a toolbox of leadership styles that can be used with different people and in different situations. However, we can learn something about good leadership from each of the animal examples. We can also learn a lot about what to avoid.

As quoted in the start of this chapter, popular science writer Stephen Jay Gould says: 'Why should nastiness be the baggage of an apish past and our kindness uniquely human? Why should we not seek continuity with other animals for our 'noble' traits as well?' We have all seen popular literature that compares us with Chimpanzees, using our animal natures to explain greed, aggression and unkindness in humans. 'We can't help it. It is our animal instincts.' But, as we have also seen, chimps control aggression, reconcile, will not tolerate an unfair leader and strategise complex alliances. As animal cousins they are also only one part of our genetic family. We also have Bonobos as equally close relatives – relatives who operate in a much kinder society.

Successful long-term leaders in animal societies have the following characteristics:
• They are trustworthy.
• They keep the group safe.
• They resolve conflict quickly.
• They make productive decisions for the group.
• They share resources fairly.
• They have compassion and empathy.

These traits are present in our primate cousins, the Bonobos and Chimpanzees – they are character traits we can potentially trace back to our common evolutionary ancestor. Researchers have asked the question: are we more like Bonobos or Chimpanzees? The jury is still out on a definitive answer. Perhaps we will know one day. Meanwhile, Frans de Waal, who has worked closely with both species, calls us humans the 'bi-polar ape'. We have a bit of Bonobo and a bit of Chimpanzee in all of us. There is an ape blueprint for a range of conduct from despotic to altruistic. The choice is ours over which to bring to the fore. We are capable of unconditional love, kindness, empathy and altruism. We can be good and fair leaders, in our families, workplaces, communities, even globally. We are the only species that can do so to ameliorate climate change, to slow unsustainable population growth and to halt the extinction of precious animal species for whom time is running out.

Perhaps we can do so by channelling our *best* inner ape.

ACKNOWLEDGEMENTS

The books and articles of my fellow Dutchman Frans de Waal have been an inspiration throughout my career. With each book and research paper he has been able to highlight a different angle of the inner lives of wild animals. For those of us who are privileged to work with wild animals every day, each book has brought the proof of what we thought we saw. His research has helped us to understand our primate cousins and to understand ourselves better in the process. Without Frans' research, books and other writings I would not have the conviction to write this book.

Further impetus to write this book came from Andrew Nicolaidis and Emma Pollard who asked me to develop a workshop for Taronga Zoo based on 'What We Can Learn From Wild Animals About Leadership'. The thought of writing a book on this topic had been floating in my head for a while. Developing the workshop helped me focus on the topic for long enough to get me in the right frame of mind and start writing.

Many people gave their time to tell me stories about the animals they work with and gave permission to share these with you. I am grateful for their willingness to impart their tales. My sincere thanks to Allan Schmidt, Simon Duffy, Amanda Everett, Lucy Melo, Louise Ginman, Neil Jordan, Pascale Benoit, Jordan Michelmore, Karen Fifield, Jo Richardson, Harmony Neale, Melissa Shipway and Elle Bombonato. Several of these lovely people and others also read an early draft chapter for me: Allan Schmidt, Neil Jordan, Vera Nedved, Lucy Melo, Louise Ginman and Anna Bennett made a great contribution to some of the more subtle intricacies of the leadership behaviour of several species.

Thanks to Sara Brice for her help in finding some historic information on a couple of animals. My thanks to Lisa Keen for discussions on protocol. Thanks to Paul Andrew for heated and interesting discussions on many topics including this one.

As one does on a long project, I lost confidence at times and the coaching by Jo Riccioni got me back on track each time. I am grateful for her review of an early draft and thank her for her invaluable encouragement and feedback with respect to scope, structure and style.

Many helpful comments were made by the reviewers of an early draft by Max Elliott, Derek Spielman and Laurie Bradley. My husband Rob ploughed through some very rough text early on and gave me some solid feedback, made lots of cups of tea and tolerated my writing obsession with good grace. Any omissions or mistakes are obviously entirely mine. I owe each of these primates a debt of gratitude.

Thank you to all at New Holland, including Publisher Simon Papps, Editor Xavier Waterkeyn and Designer Sean Robertson.

Last but not least, cheers to all the animals that have intrigued and inspired me throughout my life. They made me laugh and made me cry. Sometimes I cried because they bit, scratched or kicked me but I can never repay the privilege of being in their lives. I hope that in some way the portraits painted in this book help to give them the respect and protection they deserve.

SOURCES

This book is intended for a general readership and those interested in leadership. I have therefore not quoted references directly in the text. Interested readers can find the books, articles and papers that provided information and inspiration listed below.

INTRODUCTION

de Waal, F. (2007). *Chimpanzee Politics: power and sex among apes* (25th Anniversary edition). John Hopkins University Press.

1. THE HUMAN ANIMAL

Cocks, L. (2016). *Orangutans, My Cousins, My Friends*. The Orangutan Project.

Colon, C.P. and Campos-Arceiz, A. (2013). 'The impact of gut passage by Binturongs (*Arctictis binturong*) on seed germination.' *The Raffles Bulletin of Zoology* 61 (1): 417–421.

Darwin, C. (2011). *The Descent of Man*. Madison Park. Pacific Publishing Studio.

Dunbar, R. (2004). *The Human Story; A New History of Mankind's Evolution*. Faber and Faber, London.

Dunbar, R. (1998). *Grooming, Gossip and the Evolutionary Language*. Faber and Faber, London.

Gonzalez Forero, M. and Gardner, A. (2018). 'Inference of ecological and social drivers of human brain-size evolution.' *Nature* 557 (7706): 554–557. DOI: 10.1038/s41586-018-0127-x

Goodall, J. (1971). *In the Shadow of Man*. Dell Publishing Co., Inc.

Harari, Y.N. (2014). *Sapiens: A Brief History of Humankind*. Penguin Random House.

Lindburg, D.G. and Baragona, K. (2004). *Giant Pandas: Biology and Conservation*. University of California Press.

Morris, D. (2017). *The Naked Ape* (50th Anniversary Edition). Vintage Penguin Books.

Sahu, M. and Prasuna, J.G. (2016). Twin Studies: A Unique Epidemiological Tool. *Indian Journal of Community Medicine: Official Publication of Indian Association of Preventive & Social Medicine* 41 (3): 177–182. doi. org/10.4103/0970-0218.183593

Sapolsky, R. (2017). *Behave: The Biology of Humans at Our Best and Worst*. Penguin Random House.

Sockol, M.D., Raichlen, D.A. and Pontzer, H. (2007). 'Chimpanzee locomotor energetics and the origin of human bipedalism.' *Proceedings National Academy of Sciences 104 (30): 12265–12269.*

de Waal, F. (2005). *Our Inner Ape: The Best and Worst of Human Nature*. Granta Books.

Wright, R. (2004). *A Short History of Progress*. The Text Publishing Company.

Websites

Hall, A. (2015). Healthy living: Your Active Social Life Could Help You Live Longer. *HuffPost*, 18 July 2015. Downloaded 15.5.2018.

Loos, I. The Political Philosophy of Aristotle, *The Annals of the American Academy of Political and Social Science*, Vol. 10 (Nov. 1897), pp. 1–21, Sage Publications: www.jstor.org/stable/1009646 Downloaded 21.4.2018.

Resnick, B. 'Why do humans have such huge brains? Scientists have a few hypotheses. Congrats, you have an enormous brain! (For a primate.) Scientists are trying to figure out why,' *Vox*, May 2018. www.vox.com/science-and-health/2018/5/23/17377200/human-brain-size-evolution-nature Downloaded 30.6.2018.

Troyer, A.K. The health benefits of socialising. *Psychology Today.* www.psychologytoday.com/us/blog/living-mild-cognitive-impairment/201606/the-health-benefits-socializing. Downloaded 15.4.2018.

2. TEAMWORK IN ANIMALS

Anderson, C. and Franks, N.R. (2001). 'Teams in animal societies'. *Behavioral Ecology* 12, 5: 534–540.

Clutton-Brock, T. (2008). *Meerkat Manor; Flower of the Kalahari.* Phoenix.

Conradt, L. and Roper, T.J. (2007). 'Democracy in animals: evolution of shared group decisions.' *Proceedings of the Royal Society B.* DOI: 10.1098/rspb.2007.0186

Dunbar R. (1996). *Grooming, Gossip and the Evolutionary Language.* Harvard Press, USA.

Feinberg, M., Willer, R. and Schultz, M. (2014). 'Gossip and Ostracism Promote Cooperation in Groups.' *Psychological Science* 25 (3).

Morris, D. (2017). *The Naked Ape* (50th Anniversary Edition). Vintage Penguin Books.

Nowak, R.M. and Paradiso, J.L. (1983). *Walker's Mammals of the World* (4th Edition). Johns Hopkins University Press.

Petit, O., Gautrais, J., Leca, J.B., Theraulaz, G. and Deneubourg, J.L. (2009). 'Collective Decision Making in White-faced Capuchin Monkeys.' *Proceedings of the Royal Society B.* DOI: 10.1098/rspb.2009.0983

Sinek, S. (2011). *Start with Why*. Penguin Putnam Inc.

Sinek, S. (2017). *Why Leaders eat last: Why some teams pull together and others don't.* Penguin Random House.

Von Frisch, K. (1967). *The Dance Language and Orientation of Bees.* Harvard University Press.

de Waal, F. (2005). *Our Inner Ape: The Best and Worst of Human Nature.* Granta Books.

de Waal, F. (2007). *Chimpanzee Politics: power and sex among apes* (25th Anniversary edition). Johns Hopkins University Press.

Walker, R.H., King, A.J., McNutt, J.W., and Jordan, N.R. (2017). 'Sneeze to leave: African Wild Dogs (*Lycaon pictus*) use variable quorum thresholds facilitated by sneezes in collective decisions.' *Proceedings of the Royal Society B*. DOI: 10.1098/rspb.2017.0347

Websites

African Proverb. Quote: If you want to go fast, go alone. If you want to go far, go together. www.passiton.com/inspirational-quotes/7293-if-you-want-to-go-fast-go-alone-if-you-want Downloaded 25.9.2018.

Hirata, S., Watanabe, K. and Kawai, M. 'Sweet-Potato Washing Revisited.' *Japan Monkey Centre*. www.japanmonkeycentre.org/pdf/sweet-potato-washing/Hirata-2001-Sweet-potato-washing-revisited.pdf Downloaded 25.9.2018.

Watson, S.K., Townsend, S.W., Schel, A.M., Wilke, C., Wallace, E.K., Cheng, L., West, V. and Slocombe, K.E., 'Vocal Learning in the Functionally Referential Food Grunts of Chimpanzees.' *Current Biology*, Published Online: 5 February 2015. www.cell.com/current-biology/fulltext/S0960-9822 (14)01635-2 Downloaded 14.4.2018.

3. A NATURAL HISTORY OF LEADERSHIP

Barger, N., Hanson, K.L., Teffer, K., Schenker-Ahmed, N.M. and Semendeferi K. (2014). 'Evidence for evolutionary specialization in human limbic structures.' *Frontiers in Human Neuroscience* 8: 277. DOI: 10.3389/fnhum.2014.00277

Boehm, C. (1999). *Hierarchy in the Forest – The Evolution of Egalitarian Behaviour*. Harvard University Press.

Dunbar R. (1996). *Grooming, Gossip and the Evolutionary Language*. Harvard Press, USA.

Gallup, G.G. (1970). 'Chimpanzees: Self recognition.' *Science* 167 (3914): 86–7

Giphart, R. and van Vugt, M. (2018). *Mismatch: How Our Stone Age Brain Deceives Us Every Day (and What We Can Do About It)*. Robinson.

Hare, B., Call, J., Agnetta, B. and Tomasello, M. (2000). 'Chimpanzees know what conspecifics do and do not see.' *Animal Behaviour* 59 (4): 771–785. DOI:10.1006/anbe.1999.1377

Hogan, R. (2006). *Personality and the fate of organizations*. Hillsdale, NJ: Erlbaum.

LeDoux, J.E. (2015). 'Feelings: What Are They and How Does The Brain Make Them?' *American Academy of Arts and Sciences* 144 (1). DOI: 10.1162/DAED_a_00319

Krupenye, C., Kano, F., Hirata, S., Call, J. and Tomasello, M. (2016). 'Great apes anticipate that other individuals will act according to false beliefs.' *Science* 354 (6308): 110–114. DOI:10.1126/science.aaf8110

Nowak, R.M. and Paradiso, J.L. (1983). *Walker's Mammals of the World* (4th Edition). Johns Hopkins University Press.

Smith, J.E., Gavrilets, S., Borgerhoff Mulder, M., Hooper, P.L., El Mouden, C., Nettle, D., Hauert, C., Hill, K., Perry, S., Pusey, A.E., van Vugt, M. and Alden Smith, E. (2016). 'Leadership in Mammalian Societies: Emergence, Distribution, Power, and Payoff.' *Trends in Ecology and Evolution* 31 (1):

54–66. DOI-org.ezproxy.lib.uts.edu.
au/10.1016/j.tree.2015.09.013

Stulp, G., Buunk, A.P., Verhulst, S., and
Pollet, T.V. (2013). 'Tall claims? Sense
and nonsense about the importance
of height of US presidents.' *The
Leadership Quarterly*, 24 (1). DOI.
org/10.1016/j.leaqua.2012.09.002

van Vugt, M. (2006). 'Evolutionary
Origins of Leadership and
Followership.' *Personality and Social
Psychology Review* 10 (4): 354–371.

van Vugt, M., Hogan, R. and Kaiser, R.
(2008). 'Leadership, followership,
and evolution: Some lessons from
the past.' *American Psychologist* 63:
182–196.

de Waal, F. (2005). *Our Inner Ape: The
Best and Worst of Human Nature*.
Granta Books.

de Waal, F. (2009). *The Age of
Empathy: Nature's Lessons for a
Kinder Society*. Three Rivers Press.

de Waal, F. (2016). *Are We Smart
Enough to Know How Smart Animals
Are*. Granta Books.

Websites

Link, CH.C. (1921). 'Emotions and
Instincts.' *The American Journal of
Psychology* 32 (1): 134–144. Stable
URL: www.jstor.org/stable/1413480.
Downloaded 14.6.2018.

Tooby, J. and Cosmides, L. 'Evolutionary
psychology: a primer.' *Centre for
Evolutionary Psychology*.
http:/www.cep.ucsb.edu/primer.htlm.
Downloaded 15.6.2018.

Xue, Z., Zhang, W., Wang, L., Hou, R.,
Zhang, M., Fei, L., Zhang, X., Huang,
H., Bridgewater, L.C., Jiang, Y., Jiang,

C., Zhao, L., Pang, X. and Zhang, Z.,
(2015). 'The Bamboo-Eating Giant
Panda Harbors a Carnivore-Like Gut
Microbiota, with Excessive Seasonal
Variations.' *American Society for
Microbiology*, mBio. 6, 3 e00022-15.
DOI: 19 May 2015.

2018 Darwin Awards, Honoring
Charles Darwin, the father of
evolution, commemorates those who
improve our gene pool-by removing
themselves from it. darwinawards.
com/darwin/darwin2018-06.html
Downloaded 25.9.2018.

4. THE AUTHORITARIAN LEADER

Bright, M. (2000). *Gorillas: the Greatest
Apes*, BBC.

Grossfeldt, L. and Blissett, D. (2015). *Our
Primate Family: Stories of Conservation
and Kin*. Melbourne Books.

Harcourt, A.H. and Stewart K.J. (2007).
*Gorilla Society: Conflict, Compromise
and Cooperation Between the Sexes*.
University of Chicago Press.

Nowak, R.M. and Paradiso, J.L. (1983).
Walker's Mammals of the World (4th
Edition). Johns Hopkins University
Press.

Cragen, J.F., Wright, D.W. and Kasch,
C.R. (2009). *Communication in Small
Groups: Theory, Process, and Skills*.
Wadsworth.

Daft, R.L. (2015). *The Leadership
Experience*. Stamford, CT: Cengage
Learning.

Websites

About.com: Psychology. What is
Authoritarian Leadership? (2013).
psychology.about.com/od/

leadership/f/autocratic-leadership. htm
Downloaded 23.4.2018.

Authoritarian countries. www.governmentvs.com/en/ authoritarian-countries/model-57-4. Downloaded 25.5.2018.

Authoritarian leadership: Use Sparingly. www.educational-business-articles-com/authoritarian-leadership/ Downloaded 12.3.2018.

Darwin, C. Quote. www.goodreads. com/quotes/476991-besides-love-and-sympathy-animals-exhibit-other-qualities-connected-with Downloaded 25.9.2018.

Dunk, M., 'A mother's grief: Heartbroken gorilla cradles her dead baby', *Daily Mail On-line*, 19 August 2008. www.dailymail.co.uk/sciencetech/ article-1046549/A-mothers-grief-Heartbroken-gorilla-cradles-dead-baby. html#ixzz5DMM6eN6e Downloaded 23.3.2018.

Hanno the Navigator. 'A Carthaginian Exploration of the West African Coast'. *www.shsu.edu/~his_ncp/ Hanno.html* Downloaded 26 .5.2018.

King Kong the Movie. King Kong, American Film Institute: catalog.afi. com/Catalog/moviedetails/4005. Downloaded 26.5.2018.

Gorilla Myths and Legends: www. rozhlas.cz/therevealed/comments/_ zprava/247925. Downloaded 25.5.2018.

Leadership Toolbox: www.leadership-toolbox.com/autocratic-leadership. html Downloaded 23.4.2018.

Maisels, F., Strindberg, S., Breuer, T., Greer, D., Jeffery, K. and Stokes, E. (2016). *Gorilla gorilla* ssp. *gorilla*. The IUCN Red List of Threatened Species 2016: e.T9406A102328866. dx.doi. org/10.2305/IUCN.UK.2016-2.RLTS. T9406A17989591.en. Downloaded 25.5.2018.

Shimbun, C. 'Good-looking gorilla has crowds going gaga at Higashiyama Zoo.' *Japanese Times*. www. japantimes.co.jp/news/2015/06/29/ national/good-looking-gorilla-crowds-going-gaga-higashiyama-zoo/#. W6mbtkkUnIU Downloaded 25.9.2018.

5. THE ADAPTABLE LEADER

Couzin, I.D. (2006). 'Behavioral Ecology: Social Organization in Fission–Fusion Societies.' *Current Biology* 16 (5): 169–171. DOI: 10.1016/j. cub.2006.02.042

East, M.L., Burke, T., Wilhelm, K., Greig, C. and Hofer, H. (2003). 'Sexual conflicts in Spotted Hyena; male and female mating tactics and their reproductive outcome with respect to age, social status and tenure.' *Proceedings of the Royal Society of London B*. 270: 1247–1254.

Holekamp, K.E., Sakai, S.T. and Lundrigan, B.L. (2007). 'Social intelligence in the Spotted Hyena (*Crocuta crocuta*)' *Philosophical Transactions of the Royal Society B* 362 (1480); 523–538.

Holekamp, K.E., Sakai, S.T. and Lundrigan, B.L. (2007). 'The Spotted Hyena (*Crocuta crocuta*) as a Model System for the Study of the Evolution of Intelligence.' *Journal of Mammology* 88, 3. DOI. org/10.1644/06-MAMM-S-361R1.1

Kemper, S. (2008). 'Who's Laughing Now? 'Long maligned as nasty scavengers, hyenas turn out to be protective parents and accomplished hunters.' *Smithsonian Magazine*.

Kruuk, H. (1972). *The Spotted Hyena; a Study of Predation and Social Behaviour.* The University of Chicago Press.

Martel, Y. (2001). *The Life of Pi.* Seal Books.

Montgomery, S. and Bishop, N. (2018). *The Hyena Scientist.* Houghton Mifflin Harcourt.

Smale, L., Holekamp, K.E. and White, P.A. (1999). 'Siblicide revisited in the spotted hyaena: does it conform to obligate or facultative models?' *Animal Behaviour* 58: 545–551.

Smith, J.E., Estrada, J.R., Richards, H.R., Dawes, S.E., Mitsos, K. and Holekamp, K.E. (2015). 'Collective movements, leadership and consensus costs at reunions in spotted hyaenas.' *Animal Behaviour* 105: 187–200. DOI: 10.1016/j. anbehav.2015.04.023

Wahaj, S.A., Guse, K. and Holekamp, K.E. (2001). 'Reconciliation in the Spotted Hyena (*Crocuta crocuta*).' *Ethology* 107: 1057–1074.

Websites

Blake, M. (2014). 'Zoo abandons Hyena breeding programme after realising they have spent four years trying to get two males to mate.' *Daily Mail Australia*, 4 October 2014. www.dailymail.co.uk/news/article-2779655/Zookeepers-Japan-abandon-year-long-attempt-make-two-spotted-hyenas-mate-realise-MALE.html Downloaded 22.6.2018.

Boss, J. (2015). 'Three Characteristics of Adaptive Thinkers.' *Forbes.* www.forbes.com/sites/jeffboss/2015/07/01/3-characteristics-of-adaptive-thinkers/#3b8fd781e179 Downloaded 18.6.2018.

Nicholls, H. (2014). 'The Truth About Spotted Hyenas.' *BBC.* www.bbc.com/earth/story/20141028-the-truth-about-spotted-hyenas. Downloaded 1.7.18.

Torres, R., and Rimmer, N. (2011). 'The Five Traits of Highly Adaptive Leadership Teams, What Senior Leaders Do Differently.' *The Boston Consulting Group.* www.bcg.com/en-au/publications/2011/people-organization-five-traits-highly-adaptive-leadership-teams.aspx Downloaded 18.6.2018.

6. THE LAISSEZ-FAIRE LEADER

Chauvet, J-M., Brunel, D.E. and Hillaire, C. (1996). *Dawn of Art: The Chauvet Cave. The oldest known paintings in the world.* Harry N. Abrams.

Cragen, J.F., Wright, D.W. and Kasch, C.R. (2009). *Communication in Small Groups: Theory, Process and Skills.* Wadsworth Cengage Learning.

Fei, F.C. (ed.) (2002). *Chinese Theories of Theater and Performance from Confucius to the Present.* University of Michigan Press.

Gibbs, L. (2002). *Aesop's Fables* (Oxford World's Classics), Oxford University Press.

Garai, J. (1973). *The Book of Symbols*. Simon and Schuster, New York.

Leroi-Gourhan, A. and Allain J. (1979). *Lascaux inconnu. XXIIe supplement à 'Gallia Préhistoire'*. Paris.

Hogarth, C. and Butler, N. (2004). 'Animal Symbolism (Africa)'. In Walter, M.N., *Shamanism: An Encyclopedia of World Beliefs, Practices and Culture*, 1: 3–6. ABC Clio.

Novak, R.M. (1999). *Walker's Mammals of the World*. 6th Edition. Johns Hopkins University Press.

Stander, P.E. (1992). 'Cooperative Hunting in Lions: The Role of the Individual.' *Behavioral Ecology and Sociobiology* 29 (6): 445–454. www.jstor.org/stable/4600646

Sunquist, M., and Sunquist, F. (2002). *Wild Cats of the World*. University of Chicago Press.

Tressider, J. (1997). *The Hutchinson Dictionary of Symbols*. Helicon Publishers.

Websites

Bauer, H., Packer, C., Funston, P.F., Henschel, P. and Nowell, K. (2016). *Panthera leo* (errata version published in 2017). The IUCN Red List of Threatened Species 2016: e.T15951A115130419. dx.doi.org/10.2305/IUCN.UK.2016-3.RLTS.T15951A107265605.en. Downloaded 14.4.2018.

The Lion Centre. University of Minnesota, College of Biological Sciences. cbs.umn.edu/research/labs/lionresearch Downloaded 15.5.2018.

Weaver, J. Quote: A lioness has got a lot more power than the lion likes to think she has. Read more at: www.brainyquote.com/quotes/jacki_weaver_516975?src=t_lion Downloaded 14.5.2018.

7. THE DEMOCRATIC LEADER

Conradt, L and Roper, T.J. (2003). 'Group decision-making in animals.' *Nature* 9, 421 (6919): 155–8.

Conradt, L and Roper, T.J. (2007). 'Democracy in Animals: The Evolution of Shared Group Decisions.' *Proceedings of the Royal Society B: Biological Sciences* 274 (1623): 2317–2326.

Conradt, L. and Roper, T.J. (2009). 'Conflicts of interest and the evolution of decision sharing.' *Phil. Trans. R. Soc. B* 364: 807–819. DOI: 10.1098/rstb.2008.0257.

Hall, K. and DeVore, I. (1965). 'Baboon Social Behaviour', in DeVore, I. (ed.) *Primate Behaviour*. Holt.

Jorge, P.E. and Marques, P.A.M. (2012). 'Decision-making in pigeon flocks: a democratic view of leadership.' *Journal of Experimental Biology* 215: 2414–2417. DOI: 10.1242/jeb.070375

List, C. (2004). 'Democracy in animal groups: a political science perspective.' *Trends in Evolution* 19 (4): 168–169. doi.org/10.1016/j.tree.2004.02.004

Martindale, N. (2001). 'Leadership styles: How to handle the different personas.' *Strategic Communication*

Management 15(8): 32–35.

Prins, H.H.T. (1996). *Ecology and behaviour of the African buffalo.*

Chapman Sapolsky, R.M. (2002). *A Primate's Memoir.* Vintage.

Strandburg-Peshkin, A., Farine, D.R., Couzin, I.D. and Crofoot, M.C. (2015). 'Shared decision-making drives collective movement in wild baboons', *Science* 348 (6241): 1358–1361. DOI: 10.1126/science.aaa5099

Wang, X., Sun, L., Li, J., Xia, D., Sun, B. and Zhang, D. (2015). 'Collective Movement in the Tibetan Macaques (*Macaca thibetana*): Early Joiners Write the Rule of the Game.' *PLoS ONE* 10 (5): e0127459. doi.org/10.1371/journal.pone.0127459

Websites

Bovard, J. Quote: Democracy must be something more than two wolves and a sheep voting on what to have for dinner. www.goodreads.com/work/quotes/977235-lost-rights-the-destruction-of-american-liberty. Downloaded 19.7.2018.

Cherry, K., (2018). 'What is Democratic leadership? Characteristics, benefits, drawbacks and famous examples', *Very Well Mind.* www.verywellmind.com/what-is-democratic-leadership-2795315 Downloaded 25.6.2018.

Gill, E. (2016). St. Thomas University Online. 'What is Democratic/Participative Leadership? How Collaboration Can Boost Morale.' online.stu.edu/articles/education/democratic-participative-leadership.aspx

Downloaded 27.6.2018

Leadership Central, 'Overview of Democratic Leadership Style'. www.leadership-central.com/democratic-leadership-style.html#axzz5JbTpWIoQ. Downloaded 26.6.2018

Sun, L. (2017). 'Would Twitter Ruin Bee Democracy? Simple-majority democracy is used by many animals. But they don't have social media.' nautil.us/issue/55/trust/would-twitter-ruin-bee-democracy Downloaded 25.6.18.

8. THE MATERNALISTIC LEADER

Cohen, A.A.F. (2004). 'Female post-reproductive lifespan: a general mammalian trait.' *Biol. Rev. Camb. Philos. Soc.* Nov. 79 (4): 733–50.

Ellis, S., Franks, D.W., Nattrass, S., Cant, M., Bradley, D.L., Giles, D., Balcomb, K. and Croft, D.P. (2018). 'Post-reproductive lifespans are rare in mammals.' *Ecology and Evolution* 1 (13).

Garstang M, Davis RE, Leggett K, Frauenfeld OW, Greco S, Zipser E, et al. (2014). 'Response of African Elephants (*Loxodonta africana*) to Seasonal Changes in Rainfall.' *PLoS ONE* 9(10): e108736. doi.org/10.1371/journal.pone.0108736

Guading, M. (2009). *The signs and symbols bible: the definitive guide to mysterious markings.* New York: Sterling Pub. Co.

Lemieux, A.M. and Clarke, R.V. (2009). 'The International ban on ivory sales and its effects on elephant poaching in Africa.' *Brit. J. Criminol.* 49: 451–471. doi:10.1093/bjc/azp030

Meredith, M. (2001). *Africa's Elephant; a biography.* Hodder and Stoughton, London.

Moss, C. (2000). *Elephant Memories.* University of Chicago.

Lee, P.C., Fishlock, V., Webber, C.E., and Moss, C.J. (2016). The reproductive advantages of a long life: longevity and senescence in wild female African elephants. *Behavioral Ecology and Sociobiology* 70: 337–345. doi. org/10.1007/s00265-015-2051-5

Binney, R. (2006). *Nature's Ways Lore, Legend, Fact and Fiction.* F+W Media.

McComb, K., Shannon, G., Durant, S., Sayialel, K., Slotow, R., Poole, J. and Moss, C. (2011). 'Leadership in elephants: the adaptive value of age.' *Proceedings of the Royal Society B: Biological Sciences* 278 (1722): 3270–3276. DOI: 10.1098/rspb.2011.0168

de Silva, S. and Wittemyer, G. (2012). 'A comparison of social organisation in Asian Elephants and African Savanna Elephants.' *International Journal of Primatology* 33: 1125–1141. DOI: 10.1007/s10764-011-9564-1

de Silva, S., Ranjeewa, A.D.G. and Kryazhimskiy, S. (2011). 'The dynamics of social networks among female Asian Elephants.' *BMC Ecology* 11:17.

de Silva, S., Schmid, V. and Wittemyer G. (2017). 'Fission–fusion processes weaken dominance networks of female Asian Elephants in a productive habitat.' *Behavioral Ecology* 28 (1): 243–252. DOI:10.1093/beheco/arw153

Wijayagunawardane, M.P.B., Short, R.V.,

Samarakone, T.S., Madhuka Nishany, K.B., Harrington, H., Perera, B.V.P., Rassool, R. and Bittner, E.P. (2016). 'The use of audio playback to deter crop-raiding Asian Elephants.' *Wildlife Society Bulletin.* DOI: 10.1002/wsb.652

Websites

Blanc, J. (2008). *Loxodonta africana.* The IUCN Red List of Threatened Species 2008: e.T12392A3339343. dx.doi.org/10.2305/IUCN.UK.2008. RLTS.T12392A3339343.en. Downloaded 29.4.2018.

ConnectUS. '17 Advantages and Disadvantages of Paternalistic Leadership.' connectusfund.org/17-advantages-and-disadvantages-of-paternalistic-leadership Downloaded 28.4.2018.

Choudhury, A., Lahiri Choudhury, D.K., Desai, A., Duckworth, J.W., Easa, P.S., Johnsingh, A.J.T., Fernando, P., Hedges, S., Gunawardena, M., Kurt, F., Karanth, U., Lister, A., Menon, V., Riddle, H., Rübel, A. and Wikramanayake, E. (IUCN SSC Asian Elephant Specialist Group). (2008). *Elephas maximus.* The IUCN Red List of Threatened Species 2008: e.T7140A12828813. dx.doi. org/10.2305/IUCN.UK.2008.RLTS. T7140A12828813.en. Downloaded 29.4.2018.

Darwin, C. Quote: 'The Indian Elephant is said sometimes to weep.' Famous Quotes and Quotations. www. quotesquotations.com/find/quotes-about-elephants.htm Downloaded 25.9.2018.

Fishlock, V. (2011). 'Why Matriarchs

Matter in Elephant Society. ' IFAW.
www.ifaw.org/united-states/
node/2842
Downloaded 23.4.2018.

Leadership Resource Center.
'Paternalistic Leadership Approach
– What Is It and Is It Outdated?'
leadertoday.org/faq/paternalistic.htm
Downloaded 28.4.2018.

Martin 'Paternalistic Leadership Guide:
Definition, Qualities, Pros and Cons,
Examples.' *Cleverism*. August 15, 2016.
www.cleverism.com/paternalistic-
leadership-guide/
Downloaded 28.4.2018.

O'Connell-Rodwell, C. (2010). 'How
Male Elephants Bond.' *Smithsonian
Magazine*, November 2010.
Downloaded 14.7.2018.

9. THE POLITICAL LEADER

Goodall, J. (1971). *In the Shadow of Man.*
Dell Publishing Co.

Hare, B., Melis, A.P., Woods, V.,
Hastings, S. and Wrangham, R.
(2007). 'Tolerance Allows Bonobos
to Outperform Chimpanzees
on a Cooperative Task.' *Current
Biology* 17: 619–623. DOI: 0.1016/j.
cub.2007.02.040.

Diamond, J.M. (1993). *The Third
Chimpanzee: The Evolution and
Future of the Human Animal.* Harper
Perennial.

*Gibbons, A. (2012). 'Bonobos Join
Chimps as Closest Human Relatives.'
Science,* American Association for
the Advancement of Science. 13 June
2012.

Gilby, I.C., Brent, L.J.N., Wroblewski,

E.E., Rudicell, R. S., Hahn, B.H.,
Goodall, J. and Pusey, A.E. (2012).
'Fitness benefits of coalitionary
aggression in male Chimpanzees.'
Behavioral Ecology and Sociobiology,
67 (3): 373–381. DOI: 10.1007/s00265-
012-1457-6

Laporte, N.C. and Zuberbuhler, K.V
(2010). 'Vocal greeting behaviour in
wild Chimpanzee females.' *Animal
Behaviour* 80 (3): 467–473. doi.
org/10.1016/j.anbehav.2010.06.005

Varki, N., Anderson, D., Herndon, J.G.,
Pham, T., Gregg, C.J., Cheriyan,
M., Murphy, J., Strobert, E., Fritz,
J., Else, J.G. and Vark, A. (2009).
'Heart disease is common in
humans and Chimpanzees, but is
caused by different pathological
processes.' *Evolutionary Application*s
2 (1): 101–112. DOI: 10.1111/j.1752-
4571.2008.00064.

de Waal, F. (2005). *Our Inner Ape: The
Best and Worst of Human Nature.*
Granta Books.

de Waal, F. (2007). *Chimpanzee
Politics: power and sex among apes*
(25th Anniversary Edition). Johns
Hopkins University Press.

Walker, A. (2009). 'The Strength
of Great Apes and the Speed of
Humans.' *Current Anthropology* 50
(2): 229. DOI: 10.1086/592023

Wittig, R.M. and Boesch, C. (2003).
'Food competition and linear
dominance hierarchy among Female
Chimpanzees of the Taï National Park.'
International Journal of Primatology
24 (4).

Wong, K. (2014). 'Tiny Genetic
Differences between Humans and

Other Primates Pervade the Genome.' *Scientific American*. 2 September 2014.

Websites

Goodall, J. Quote: Chimps are very quick to have a sudden fight or aggressive episode, but they're equally as good at reconciliation. www.brainyquote.com/quotes/jane_goodall_471138 Downloaded 30.6.2018.

The Jane Goodall Institute. Chimpanzees Don't Make Good Pets. web.archive.org/web/20150202195221/www.janegoodall.org/chimp-central-pets Downloaded 9.5.2018.

10. THE EGALITARIAN LEADER

Boehm, C. (1999). *Hierarchy in the Forest – The Evolution of Egalitarian Behavior.* Harvard University Press.

Clay, Z. and de Waal, F.B.M. (2015). 'Sex and strife: post-conflict sexual contacts in Bonobos.' *Behaviour* 15 (3–4): 313–334. DOI: 10.1163/1568539X-00003155

Furuichi, T. (1989). 'Social interactions and the life history of female *Pan paniscus* in Wamba, Zaire.' *International Journal of Primatology* 10 (3): 173–197.

Furuichi, T. (1997). 'Agonistic Interactions and Matrifocal Dominance Rank of Wild Bonobos *(Pan paniscus)* at Wamba.' *International Journal of Primatology* 18 (6).

Hare, B., Melis, A.P., Woods, V.,

Hastings, S. and Wrangham, R. (2007). 'Tolerance Allows Bonobos to Outperform Chimpanzees on a Cooperative Task.' *Current Biology* 17: 619–623. DOI:10.1016/j.cub.2007.02.040, 2007

Lingomo, B. and Kimura, D. (2009). 'Taboo of Eating Bonobo among the Bongando People in the Wamba Region, Democratic Republic of Congo.' *African Study Monographs* 30 (4): 209–225.

Novak, R.M. (1999). *Walker's Mammals of the World.* 6th Edition. Johns Hopkins University Press.

Paoli, T., Tacconi, G., Borgognini Tarli, S.M. and Palagi, E. (2007). 'Influence of feeding and short-term crowding on the sexual repertoire of captive Bonobos (*Pan paniscus*).' *Annales Zoologici Fennici* 44 (2): 81–88.

Prufer, K., Munch, K. and Paabo, S. (2012). 'The Bonobo genome compared with the Chimpanzee and human genomes.' *Nature* 486: 527–531. DOI:10.1038/nature11128

Rogers, N. (2017). 'Bonobo Matriarchs Lead the Way, Old females decide when and where their tribe will travel.' *Inside Science*, March 2017.

von Rohr, C.R., Koski, S.E., Burkart, J.M., Caws, C., Fraser, O.N. and Ziltener, A. and van Schaik, C.P. (2012). 'Impartial Third-Party Interventions in Captive Chimpanzees: a Reflection of Community Concern.' *PLoS ONE* 7 (3): e32494. doi.org/10.1371/journal.pone.0032494

von Rueden, C., Michael Gurven, M., Kaplan, H., and Stieglitz, J. (2014). 'Leadership in an Egalitarian Society.'

Human Nature 25 (4): 538–66.
Springer Science+Business Media.
DOI: 10.1007/s12110-014-9213-4

Tokuyama, N. and Furuichi, T. (2016).
'Do friends help each other? Patterns
of female coalition formation
in wild Bonobos at Wamba.'
Animal Behaviour 119: 27–35. DOI.
org/10.1016/j.anbehav.2016.06.021

Tokuyama, N. and Furuichi, T.
(2017). 'Leadership of old females
in collective departures in wild
Bonobos (*Pan paniscus*) at Wamba.'
Behavioural Ecology and Sociobiology
71: 55. doi.org/10.1007/s00265-017-
2277-5

Trevor-Roberts, E., Ashkanasy, N.M. and
Kennedy, J.C. (2003). 'The Egalitarian
Leader: a Comparison of Leadership
in Australia and New Zealand.' *Asia
Pacific Journal of Management* 20:
517–540.

de Waal, F. (1995). 'Bonobo, Sex and
Society.' *Scientific American*, March
1995.

de Waal, F. (2005). *Our Inner Ape: The
Best and Worst of Human Nature.*
Granta Books.

de Waal, F. (2014). *The Bonobo and
the Atheist: in Search of Humanism
Among the Primates.* W.W. Norton &
Company.

Woods, V. (2010). *Bonobo Handshake; a
Memoir of Love and Adventure in the
Congo*, Gotham Books.

Websites

Angier, N. (10 September 2016).
'Beware the Bonds of Female
Bonobos.' *New York Times.* www.
nytimes.com/2016/09/13/science/
Bonobos-apes-matriarchy.html.
Downloaded 12.5.2018.

Attenborough, D. Quote: 'If you watch
animals objectively for any length of
time, you're driven to the conclusion
that their main aim in life is to pass on
their genes to the next generation.'
www.brainyquote.com/quotes/david_
attenborough_454694
Downloaded 5.5.2018.

Fruth, B., Hickey, J.R., André, C.,
Furuichi, T., Hart, J., Hart, T., Kuehl, H.,
Maisels, F., Nackoney, J., Reinartz, G.,
Sop, T., Thompson, J. and Williamson,
E.A. (2016). *Pan paniscus* (errata
version published in 2016). The IUCN
Red List of Threatened Species
2016: e.T15932A102331567. dx.doi.
org/10.2305/IUCN.UK.2016-2.RLTS.
T15932A17964305.en.
Downloaded 13.5.2018.

Paris Logue – Left Bank vs. Right
Bank: What's the difference? www.
parislogue.com/featured-articles/
left-bank-vs-right-bank-whats-the-
difference.html
Downloaded 29.6.2018.

11. LEADERS AND FOLLOWERS UNITED

Dunbar R. (1996). *Grooming, Gossip
and the Evolutionary Language.*
Harvard Press.

Gesquiere, L.R., Learn, N.H., Simao,
M.C.M., Onyango, P.O., Alberts, S.C.
and Altmann, J. (2011). 'Life at the
Top: Rank and Stress in Wild Male
Baboons.' *Science* (New York) 333
(6040): 357–360.

Sapolsky, R.M. (2002). *A Primate's
Memoir.* Vintage.

Sapolsky, R.M. and Share L.J.
(2004). 'A pacific culture among
wild baboons: Its emergence and
transmission.' *PLoS Biol* 2 (4) e106.
DOI:10.1371/journal.pbio.0020106
Van Vugt, M., Hogan, R., and Kaiser,
R. (2008). 'Leadership, followership,
and evolution: Some lessons from
the past.' *American Psychologist* 63:
182–196.
de Waal, F. (1989). *Peacemaking among
Primates*. Harvard University Press.
de Waal, F.B.M. (1996). *Good natured:
The origins of right and wrong
in humans and other animals.*
Cambridge University Press.

Websites
'A Brief history of people power, The
Velvet Revolution, Czechoslovakia,
1989', *Time* magazine, content.
time.com/time/photogallery/
0,29307,2042879_2227408,00.html
Downloaded 24.6.2018.
Creative Spirits, Stockmen protest for
equal wages. www.creativespirits.info/
aboriginalculture/politics/aboriginal-
people-strike-walk-off-at-wave-
hill#ixzz5JJOkK28N
Downloaded 23.6.2018.
Hyacinth, B., 'Employees don't leave
Companies, they leave Managers'.
LinkedIn, December 2017. www.
linkedin.com/pulse/employees-dont-
leave-companies-managers-brigette-
hyacinth
Downloaded 24.6.2018.
Mobile Phone Recycling Scheme at
Twycross Zoo. twycrosszoo.org/news/
mobile-phone-recycling-scheme-at-
twycross-zoo/

Downloaded 21.7.2018.
Sinek, S. Quote: Facebook, 1 February
2018.
Downloaded 25.5.2018.

12. NATURAL LEADERSHIP
Boehm, C. (1999). *Hierarchy in the
Forest – The Evolution of Egalitarian
Behavior.* Harvard University Press.
Brosnan, S.F. and de Waal, F.B.M.
(2003). 'Monkeys reject unequal pay.'
Nature 425: 297–299.
Maslow, A.H. (1943). 'A Theory of
Human Motivation.' *Psychological
Review* 50: 370–396.
Prufer, K., Munch, K. and Paabo,
S. (2012). 'The Bonobo genome
compared with the Chimpanzee
and human genomes.' *Nature* 486:
527–531. DOI:10.1038/nature11128
Sapolsky R.M., and Share L.J.
(2004). 'A pacific culture among
wild baboons: Its emergence and
transmission.' *PLoS Biol* 2(4) e106.
DOI:10.1371/journal.pbio.0020106
Smith, J.E., Gavrilets, S., Borgerhoff
Mulder, M., Hooper, P.L., El Moulden,
C., Nettle, D., Hauert, C., Hill, K., Perry,
S., Pusey, A.E., Van Vugt, M. and
Alden Smith, E. (2016). 'Leadership
in Mammalian Societies: Emergence,
Distribution, Power, and Payoff.'
Trends in Ecology and Evolution 31 (1).
van Vugt, M., Hogan, R. and Kaiser, R.
(2008). 'Leadership, followership,
and evolution: Some lessons from
the past.' *American Psychologist*, 63:
182–196.
van Vugt, M., Hart, C. M., Jepson, S. F.
and De Cremer, D. (2004). 'Autocratic

leadership in social dilemmas: a threat to group stability.' *Journal of Experimental Social Psychology* 40: 1–13.

de Waal, F.B.M. (1996). *Good natured: The origins of right and wrong in humans and other animals.* Cambridge University Press.

de Waal, F. (2005). *Our Inner Ape: The Best and Worst of Human Nature.* Granta Books.

Watson, S.K., Townsend, S.W., Schel, A.M., Wilke, C., Wallace, E.K., Cheng, L., West, V. and Slocombe, K.E. (2015). 'Vocal Learning in the Functionally Referential Food Grunts of Chimpanzees.' *Current Biology* 25 (4): 495–9. DOI: 10.1016/j.cub.2014.12.032

Websites

Chicago Tribune, 'Measuring Occupy Wall Street's impact, 5 years later', www.chicagotribune.com/news/nationworld/ct-occupy-wall-street-s-impact-20160917-story.html Downloaded 26.6.2018.

Gardner, B., Why leaders must create emotional as well as physical safety in the workplace, www.forbes.com/sites/forbescoachescouncil/2017/11/30/why-leaders-must-create-emotional-as-well-as-physical-safety-in-the-workplace/#46dbb8731780. Downloaded on 10.6.18.

Gould, S.J. Quote: 'Why should our nastiness be the baggage of an apish past and our kindness uniquely human? Why should we not seek continuity with other animals for our 'noble' traits as well?' www.goodreads.com/quotes/8169742-why-should-our-nastiness-be-the-baggage-of-an-apish Downloaded 12.6.18.

New Scientist, Meet – and hear – the world's first bilingual chimps, 5 February 2015. www.newscientist.com/article/dn26922-meet-and-hear-the-worlds-first-bilingual-chimps/71654164922DOI: doi.org/10.1016/j.tree.2015.09.013 Downloaded 20.6.2018.

YouTube Experiment which shows what happens when monkeys realise they are being treated unfairly, from Frans de Waal's TED talk is called *Two Monkeys Were Paid Unequally* and can be found on www.youtube.com/watch?v=meiU6TxysCg